HOW TO UNDERSTAND LEFT-WING POLITICAL SPIN

Secrets of a Reluctant Genius

Michael P. Clutton

How to Understand Left-Wing Political Spin

Secrets of a Reluctant Genius

Michael P. Clutton

Published by Michael Clutton, 2024.

HOW TO UNDERSTAND LEFT-WING POLITICAL SPIN

First edition. July 5, 2024.

Copyright © 2024 Michael P. Clutton.

ISBN: 979-8227212702

Written by Michael P. Clutton.

Table of Contents

Congratulations on being smart enough to explore political spin, left-wing ideologies, and media narratives. But wait—before you roll your eyes, let me assure you, this isn't another dry political diatribe. No, this is your new favorite genius, reluctantly taking on the task of unraveling the liberal myths that dominate today's discourse. And yes, we'll be having some fun along the way. Expect humor, wit, and most importantly, expect to see through the smokescreen of political rhetoric.

PLEASE NOTE: I'll be dogging the conservatives on a few topics, too. Be aware that if the facts—yes, facts—provided seem unfairly slanted against liberals, it's not my fault. They've had a lot of practice at being stupid. So, don't kill the messenger.

While our tone will be satirical and light-hearted, our mission is serious. This book aims to inform and make you think critically about politics, so you can avoid being influenced by mainstream media. We'll help you understand the tricks used in left-wing political narratives, so you can make informed decisions.

ANOTHER NOTE FOR THE POLITICALLY TIMID: Every genius secret inside is verifiable via documented records, reports, interviews, etc. A list of sources and suggested reading will be provided at the end. Don't believe everything you see or read in the mainstream media. Oh yes, I'll slip you the goods on them, also.

We'll be critiquing liberal ideologies and Democratic policies, but not in the usual droning manner. Instead, we'll employ humor and controversy to keep things lively. We'll discuss various topics, like irrational liberal thinking and funny stories about political correctness. Picture this as a masterclass in political skepticism, packed in bubble-wrap to reduce the impact.

Let's begin with a story. Imagine me, a reluctant genius, trying to make sense of a complex liberal policy that's more difficult than solving a Rubik's Cube blindfolded. It was the time I tried to navigate the intricate maze of a local government environmental regulation. You see, I just wanted to mow my lawn, but apparently, I needed a permit, an environmental impact study, and a non-GMO, gluten-free, fair-trade, organic lawnmower. After weeks of paperwork and enough bureaucratic red tape to gift-wrap the Pentagon, I realized I'd spent more time on lawn care legislation than on actual lawn care.

And that's when it hit me: if this is what passes for sensible policy, we're all in trouble.

Before we get started, a final heads-up: the first section is a list of facts and truths about our topics. Think of it as an eye-opener, a primer to get your brain in gear and ready for the ride ahead. If lists aren't your thing, feel free to skip straight to Chapter One. Bring your appetite for tasty morsels of obscure revelations; the rest of the book will be a balanced smorgasbord of insightful narratives interrupted by factual bullet points. We'll explore the fabric of political absurdities with a healthy dose of satire and wit.

So, buckle up. It's going to be an enlightening, provocative journey. By the end, you'll see through the political spin and liberal myths with the clarity of a genius—or at least, as close as possible without actually being me.

50 Shocking, Verifiable Truths The Blue Side Doesn't Want You To Know

Social Programs' Efficiency:

Billions are funneled into welfare, healthcare, and housing initiatives each year, yet poverty rates and economic mobility show minimal improvement. It's like throwing money into a bottomless pit and hoping it fills up.

Despite massive spending, many government social programs see almost no return on investment. Even though billions of dollars are spent on welfare, healthcare, and housing each year, poverty rates and economic mobility stay the same. The bureaucratic overhead consumes a significant portion of funds, leaving less for actual aid. This inefficiency isn't just a fiscal issue; it translates to real people not getting the help they need. Although intentions are good, the system's poor execution leads to a never-ending cycle of dependency without meaningful progress.

Taxation and the Rich:

The top 1% of earners already pay nearly 40% of all federal income taxes. This statistic shows wealthy people are actually making a big contribution, which goes against the belief that they're not paying their fair share. Understanding that increasing taxes on this group can cause capital flight, reduced investment, and fewer jobs is important. Merely taxing the wealthy more doesn't address the complexities of economic growth and investment, so it won't solve fiscal imbalances. Higher taxes on the wealthy can inadvertently affect the middle and lower classes through reduced economic opportunities and growth.

Economic Freedom:

Countries with greater economic freedom have higher standards of living. Economic freedom, which includes personal choice, voluntary exchange, and open markets, fosters innovation and entrepreneurship. When individuals and businesses operate without excessive government interference, economies thrive, creating more jobs and wealth. Examples include Singapore and Switzerland, which consistently rank high in economic freedom and enjoy robust economies. The correlation between economic freedom and prosperity is well-documented, debunking the myth that strict government control and regulation are necessary for economic success.

Healthcare Costs:

Government intervention in healthcare often increases costs rather than reducing them. Price controls and mandates can stifle innovation and reduce the quality of care. It's like paying more to wait longer.

Government intervention in healthcare often increases costs rather than reducing them. While intended to make healthcare more accessible, excessive regulation and government programs can lead to inefficiencies and higher prices. Administrative costs balloon, and the system becomes bogged down with bureaucracy. Price controls and mandates can stifle innovation and reduce the quality of care. Countries with heavily regulated healthcare systems often experience longer wait times and limited access to advanced treatments. In contrast, market-driven systems, with competition and consumer choice, deliver better outcomes and lower costs.

Minimum Wage Myths:

Raising the minimum wage can lead to higher unemployment rates, particularly among young and unskilled workers. Automation becomes more appealing, further displacing workers. Thanks for nothing, right?

Raising the minimum wage can lead to higher unemployment rates, particularly among young and unskilled workers. While the goal is to improve living standards, the unintended consequence is often job loss, as businesses cut positions or reduce hours to offset increased labor costs. Automation becomes more appealing, further displacing workers. Studies show that modest minimum wage increases can have limited positive effects, but significant hikes can harm the very groups they intend to help. Balancing wage policies with economic realities is crucial to avoid exacerbating unemployment and poverty.

Gun Control:

Strict gun laws don't necessarily correlate with lower crime rates. As it turns out, criminals have a track-record of not following laws.

Strict gun laws don't necessarily correlate with lower crime rates. In some cases, areas with stringent gun regulations experience higher rates of violent crime. Criminals, by definition, do not obey laws, and thus stringent regulations primarily impact law-abiding citizens, limiting their ability to defend themselves. Research from sources like the CDC and FBI shows that lawful gun ownership can deter crime. Moreover, countries with high gun ownership rates, such as Switzerland, often have low crime rates, suggesting that factors other than gun availability influence crime levels.

Climate Change:

Climate policies can have severe economic consequences without significantly impacting global temperatures. While combating climate change is essential, some policies prioritize symbolic actions over effective ones. For instance, aggressive emissions reductions in developed countries might have negligible global impact if major polluters like China and India do not follow suit. Additionally, green policies can lead to job losses in traditional energy sectors and increased energy costs, disproportionately affecting low-income households. Effective climate action should balance environmental goals with economic realities, fostering innovation without sacrificing economic stability.

Welfare Dependency:

Long-term welfare can create dependency rather than empowerment. The safety net sometimes turns into a hammock.

Long-term welfare can create dependency rather than empowerment. While intended to provide a safety net, welfare programs can sometimes discourage self-sufficiency and upward mobility. When benefits are too generous or poorly structured, they can reduce the incentive to seek employment or improve one's situation. This dependency traps individuals in a cycle of poverty, undermining the original goal of temporary assistance. Successful welfare reform should focus on education, job training, and opportunities for recipients to transition off assistance, fostering independence rather than perpetual reliance.

Education Spending:

Increased spending on education hasn't led to better student performance. Maybe money can't buy intelligence after all.

Increased spending on education hasn't led to better student performance. Despite significant investments in public education, academic outcomes in the U.S. remain stagnant compared to other developed nations. Money alone doesn't address the root causes of educational deficiencies, such as outdated teaching methods, lack of accountability, and socio-economic disparities. Effective education reform should emphasize teacher quality, curriculum relevance, and student engagement, rather than simply increasing budgets. Real improvement comes from innovative approaches and a focus on results, not just financial input.

Media Bias:

Mainstream media often exhibits a liberal bias, shaping public perception more than reflecting reality. Fair and balanced? Not so much.

Mainstream media often exhibits a liberal bias, shaping public perception more than reflecting reality. Studies have shown that major news outlets frequently present information with a slant that favors liberal viewpoints. This bias can influence public opinion and political discourse, creating an echo chamber that reinforces existing beliefs rather than challenging them. It's essential for consumers to recognize this bias and seek diverse perspectives to form well-rounded opinions. Independent and alternative media sources can provide a broader view of events and issues, countering the homogeneity of mainstream narratives.

Regulation Overload:

Excessive regulations stifle small businesses and innovation. It's like trying to run a marathon with a ball and chain.

Excessive regulations stifle small businesses and innovation. When entrepreneurs spend more time complying with bureaucratic red tape than developing their products, economic growth suffers. Small businesses, which are the backbone of the economy, often lack the resources to navigate complex regulatory landscapes. This not only hampers their growth but also discourages new ventures from starting. Overregulation can lead to higher costs, reduced competition, and limited choices for consumers. Streamlining regulations to ensure they are necessary and efficient can foster a more dynamic and competitive economic environment.

Union Power:

Unions can sometimes prioritize their interests over workers' interests. While unions have historically played a crucial role in securing workers' rights, they can also become bureaucratic entities that prioritize their power and influence over the needs of individual members. For example, rigid union rules can make it difficult to address underperformance or adapt to changing market conditions. In some cases, unions have opposed measures that would benefit the broader workforce if those measures threaten their established practices.

Balancing union power with worker flexibility and economic realities is essential for a healthy labor market.

Free Speech:

Suppression of free speech on college campuses is often justified as protecting students. This trend, known as "cancel culture," stifles open debate and intellectual diversity. When controversial speakers are dis-invited or students face backlash for expressing dissenting opinions, the very foundation of academic freedom is undermined. This environment creates echo chambers where only certain viewpoints are allowed, hindering critical thinking and robust discussion. Promoting a culture of open dialogue and respect for differing opinions is crucial for the development of well-rounded, informed individuals.

Immigration Economics:

Illegal immigration can strain public resources and lower wages for low-skilled workers. While immigration brings cultural diversity and economic benefits, illegal immigration poses significant challenges. It can increase competition for low-wage jobs, driving down wages and making it harder for legal residents to find employment. Additionally, undocumented immigrants often require public services like education and healthcare without contributing proportionally to the tax base. A balanced immigration policy should ensure border security while providing a legal pathway for immigrants to contribute economically and socially.

Voter ID Laws:

Voter ID laws are supported by a majority of Americans, yet are often portrayed as controversial. Proponents argue these laws prevent voter fraud and ensure the integrity of elections. Critics claim they disproportionately affect minorities and low-income individuals. However, studies have shown that voter ID laws do not significantly suppress voter turnout. Instead, they provide a straightforward way to verify voter identity and build public confidence in the electoral process. Ensuring that every eligible voter has access to an ID can address concerns while maintaining the integrity of elections.

Public Sector Unions:

Public sector unions can create conflicts of interest in government. Unlike private sector unions, public sector unions negotiate with government officials who may rely on their political support, leading to generous compensation and benefits packages that strain public finances. This dynamic can cause pension liabilities and budget deficits, forcing cuts to essential services or higher taxes. Transparency and accountability in public sector negotiations are necessary to ensure that the interests of taxpayers and public employees are balanced.

Gender Pay Gap:

The gender pay gap narrative often ignores factors like occupation choice and hours worked. While statistics show that women, on average, earn less than men, this gap narrows significantly when accounting for differences in education, experience, and job type. Women are more likely to take career breaks for family reasons and to work part-time, which impacts overall earnings. Promoting flexible work arrangements and supporting women in high-paying fields can address these disparities more effectively than blanket policies based on incomplete data.

Police Funding:

Defunding police can lead to increased crime rates and reduced public safety. The idea behind defunding is to reallocate resources to community services, but in practice, cutting police budgets often results in fewer officers, slower response times, and higher crime rates. Studies have shown that a well-funded police force is crucial for maintaining public safety and trust. Rather than defunding, efforts should focus on reforming police practices, improving training, and fostering community relations to ensure effective law enforcement.

Charter Schools:

Charter schools often outperform public schools, yet face significant opposition. These schools offer alternatives to traditional public education, often with innovative teaching methods and curriculums tailored to students' needs. Despite their success, charter schools are frequently criticized and face regulatory hurdles that limit their expansion. Opponents argue they divert funds from public schools, but evidence suggests that competition from charter schools can drive overall improvement in the education system. Supporting charter schools can provide more educational opportunities and drive innovation in teaching.

Renewable Energy:

The push for renewable energy sometimes overlooks its current technological and economic limitations. While transitioning to renewable sources is essential for sustainability, technologies like solar and wind are not yet capable of providing consistent, large-scale power without significant support from traditional energy sources. Additionally, the production and disposal of renewable energy components can have environmental impacts. Investments in research and development are necessary to overcome these challenges and make renewable energy a viable primary source. Balancing environmental goals with practical energy needs ensures a stable and sustainable future.

Corporate Welfare:

Big corporations often benefit from government subsidies, contrary to the anti-corporate rhetoric. While public debates focus on welfare for individuals, corporate welfare—subsidies, tax breaks, and bailouts—goes relatively unnoticed. These benefits can distort markets, favoring established giants over small businesses and startups. For example, subsidies to fossil fuel industries or agricultural giants like Monsanto skew competition and stifle innovation. Addressing corporate welfare requires transparency and equitable policies that level the playing field, promoting a fairer, more competitive economy.

Foreign Aid:

Sizeable sums of foreign aid can foster dependency rather than development. While well-intentioned, foreign aid can create a cycle where recipient countries rely on external support instead of developing sustainable economies. This dependency can stifle local industries and governments, making them less accountable to their citizens. Effective foreign aid should focus on empowering local communities, building infrastructure, and promoting self-sufficiency. By supporting education, healthcare, and economic opportunities, aid can help countries build a foundation for long-term growth and independence.

Income Inequality:

Income inequality isn't inherently bad if it results from a dynamic and growing economy. The focus should be on economic mobility—ensuring that everyone has the opportunity to improve their situation. High income inequality often indicates a healthy, competitive economy where individuals are rewarded for innovation and hard work. Policies that promote education, job training, and entrepreneurship can help reduce barriers to success. Addressing income inequality requires a nuanced approach that fosters opportunity without stifling economic dynamism.

Housing Market:

Overregulation in housing markets can drive up prices and reduce availability. Zoning laws, building codes, and environmental regulations, while important, can significantly increase the cost and complexity of building new homes. This leads to housing shortages and skyrocketing prices, particularly in urban areas. Streamlining regulations and promoting smart growth policies can help increase housing supply, making homes more affordable. Encouraging mixed-use developments and reducing red tape can foster more inclusive, vibrant communities.

Job Creation:

Private sector job creation outpaces government job programs in efficiency and sustainability. The private sector responds to market demands, creating jobs that meet real economic needs. Government job programs, while useful for short-term relief, often lack the flexibility and innovation of private enterprises. Policies that support entrepreneurship, reduce regulatory burdens, and encourage investment can stimulate job growth more effectively. By fostering a business-friendly environment, governments can help create sustainable employment opportunities.

Carbon Tax:

Implementing a carbon tax can feel like putting a Band-Aid on a broken leg—well-intentioned but ultimately missing the mark.

Carbon taxes can disproportionately affect low-income households. While aimed at reducing greenhouse gas emissions, carbon taxes increase energy costs, hitting low-income families hardest as they spend a larger portion of their income on necessities like heating and transportation. To be effective and equitable, carbon tax policies need complementary measures, such as rebates or tax credits, to offset the financial burden on vulnerable populations. Comprehensive environmental strategies should balance the need for emission reductions with economic fairness.

Trade Policies:

Protectionist trade policies can harm domestic consumers and industries. While intended to protect local jobs, tariffs and trade barriers often lead to higher prices for consumers and retaliatory measures from other countries. This can hurt industries that rely on imported materials or export their products. Free trade encourages competition, innovation, and lower prices. Promoting fair trade agreements and reducing protectionist measures can stimulate economic growth and provide more choices for consumers, benefiting the broader economy.

Healthcare Systems:

Single-payer healthcare systems often lead to longer wait times and reduced quality of care. While aiming to provide universal coverage, these systems can struggle with inefficiencies and resource constraints. Patients in countries with single-payer systems frequently face long waits for procedures and limited access to advanced treatments. Balancing public and private healthcare options can provide more timely and high-quality care. A mixed system encourages competition and innovation while ensuring that essential services remain accessible to all.

Campaign Finance:

Campaign finance reforms often fail to reduce the influence of money on politics. Despite efforts to regulate contributions and spending, money finds its way into political campaigns through loopholes and unregulated channels. Wealthy donors and special interest groups still exert significant influence. Effective reform should focus on transparency and accountability, ensuring that political donations are disclosed and monitored. Encouraging small donations and public funding options can help reduce the dominance of big money in politics.

Economic Growth:

Lower taxes and reduced regulation often spur economic growth. By allowing individuals and businesses to keep more of their earnings, lower taxes encourage investment and spending. Reducing regulatory burdens frees businesses to innovate and expand, creating jobs and increasing productivity. Historical examples, such as the economic booms following tax cuts in the 1980s and early 2000s, demonstrate the positive impact of these policies. Striking a balance between necessary regulation and economic freedom is key to fostering a thriving economy.

Green Jobs:

The promise of green jobs often falls short of reality. Dreams of green gold turn into fool's gold.

The promise of green jobs often falls short of reality. While touted as the future of the economy, the creation of green jobs hasn't always matched the hype. Many green energy projects rely heavily on government subsidies and face significant economic and technological challenges. For example, solar panel manufacturing has moved overseas, where labor is cheaper, and wind turbine maintenance jobs are often temporary and region-specific. For green jobs to become a sustainable part of the economy, significant advancements in technology and infrastructure are needed, along with policies that support, rather than distort, market dynamics.

Socialism's Track Record:

Socialist policies have consistently failed in various countries. From Venezuela to the Soviet Union, implementing socialism has led to economic collapse, scarcity, and loss of personal freedoms. The allure of equality and state control often masks the reality of inefficiency, corruption, and authoritarianism. Even in democratic countries, socialist policies can stifle innovation and economic growth. Examining historical and contemporary examples, it's clear that socialism's promises of prosperity and fairness often result in the opposite, highlighting the need for caution in adopting such policies.

It's the classic bait-and-switch: promise everyone a slice of cake, then hand out crumbs.

Military Spending:

Cuts in military spending can weaken national security. While reducing military budgets might seem like a way to free up funds for other priorities, it can lead to decreased readiness and capability. A strong military deters potential adversaries and protects national interests. Historical instances, such as the pre-World War II disarmament, show the dangers of being unprepared. It's like bringing a rubber chicken to a knife fight.

Balancing military spending with fiscal responsibility ensures that the nation remains secure without overspending. Effective defense strategies require adequate funding, efficient use of resources, and a clear understanding of global threats.

Energy Independence:

Domestic energy production enhances national security and economic stability. By reducing reliance on foreign energy sources, a country can avoid the geopolitical risks associated with energy imports. The U.S., for example, has achieved significant energy independence through advances in shale oil and gas extraction. This shift not only strengthens national security but also boosts the economy by creating jobs and reducing energy costs. Continued investment in diverse energy sources, including renewables, ensures a stable and resilient energy sector that supports economic growth and security.

Who knew that drilling for oil could be a patriotic act?

Judicial Activism:

Judicial activism can undermine democratic processes and legislative intent. When judges interpret laws based on personal or political beliefs rather than the constitution, they overstep their role. Rulings may reflect a few opinions instead of the people's will voiced by elected representatives. High-profile cases often highlight the tension between judicial interpretation and legislative intent. Ensuring that judges adhere to a strict interpretation of the law preserves the balance of power and maintains the integrity of the judicial system.

It's like having referees change the rules in the middle of a game because they don't like the score.

Public Broadcasting:

Public broadcasting often leans left in its programming and news coverage. While funded by taxpayers, public broadcasting services like NPR and PBS are frequently criticized for a liberal bias. This bias can influence public opinion and shape narratives in subtle, yet significant ways. Diverse viewpoints and balanced reporting are essential for an informed public. Supporting independent and alternative media outlets can provide a broader perspective on current events and issues, fostering a more balanced and comprehensive public discourse.

It's like having a daily dose of spinach when you asked for a balanced diet.

Healthcare Innovation:

The U.S. leads in medical innovation, often stifled by overregulation. American healthcare companies are at the forefront of developing new treatments and technologies, from groundbreaking drugs to advanced surgical techniques. However, excessive regulation can slow down the approval process and increase costs, limiting access to innovative care. Streamlining regulatory frameworks while ensuring safety can speed up innovation and bring new treatments to market faster. Encouraging a competitive, market-driven healthcare system supports continuous improvement and access to the best available care.

It's like putting a speed bump on the fast lane of a highway.

Drug Policy:

War on Drugs policies have led to mass incarceration without reducing drug abuse. Harsh penalties for drug offenses have disproportionately affected minority communities and filled prisons with non-violent offenders. Despite these efforts, drug abuse remains a significant issue. Shifting focus to treatment and prevention rather than punishment can address the root causes of drug addiction. Successful programs in countries like Portugal, which emphasize decriminalization and rehabilitation, provide models for more effective drug policies that reduce harm and support recovery.

Media Mergers:

Media mergers can limit diverse viewpoints and increase bias. As major media companies consolidate, control over news and information becomes concentrated in fewer hands. This can lead to homogenized content and a narrow range of perspectives, undermining the democratic principle of a free and diverse press. Ensuring media plurality through antitrust enforcement and supporting independent journalism can help maintain a vibrant and varied media landscape. Diverse media ownership fosters a healthier public discourse and better serves the needs of a democratic society.

It's like getting all your news from one channel that's stuck on reruns.

Fiscal Responsibility:

Balanced budgets and fiscal responsibility are rare in government spending. Chronic deficit spending leads to mounting national debt, which can have long-term economic consequences. High debt levels can crowd out private investment, lead to higher interest rates, and reduce economic growth. Fiscal responsibility requires governments to prioritize spending, eliminate waste, and create sustainable budgets. Examples from both state and national governments show that disciplined financial management can lead to economic stability and growth, providing a more secure future for all citizens.

It's like maxing out your credit cards and then wondering why you can't afford groceries.

Education Reform:

School choice and voucher programs often improve educational outcomes. These initiatives allow parents to select the best educational setting for their children, fostering competition and innovation among schools. Studies have shown that students in voucher programs often perform better academically than their peers in traditional public schools. Critics argue such programs drain resources from public schools, but evidence suggests that competition can drive overall improvement in the education system. Empowering parents with choices ensures that all children have access to high-quality education.

It's like opening a gourmet restaurant in a town full of fast-food joints—everyone ups their game.

Public Debt:

Growing public debt can burden future generations. When governments continuously spend more than they earn, they accumulate debt that must eventually be repaid. This can lead to higher taxes and reduced public services for future generations. Additionally, high levels of debt can undermine investor confidence and economic stability. Responsible fiscal policies, including balanced budgets and prudent spending, are essential to avoid passing on a financial burden to our children and grandchildren. Ensuring sustainable public finances supports long-term economic health and stability.

It's like throwing a massive party and leaving the bill for your kids to pay.

Healthcare Costs:

Tort reform could significantly reduce healthcare costs. Medical malpractice lawsuits drive up insurance premiums for healthcare providers, leading to higher overall costs for patients. Fear of litigation also encourages defensive medicine, where doctors order unnecessary tests and procedures to protect themselves from potential lawsuits. Implementing tort reform can lower malpractice insurance costs and reduce the incentive for defensive medicine, ultimately decreasing healthcare expenses for everyone. Balanced legal protections and fair compensation for genuine malpractice cases can create a more efficient and cost-effective healthcare system.

Farm Subsidies:

Farm subsidies often go to large agribusinesses rather than small farmers. While intended to support struggling farmers, most subsidies benefit large agricultural corporations. This creates an uneven playing field, making it harder for small, independent farmers to compete. Additionally, these subsidies can distort market prices and lead to overproduction of certain crops. Reforming farm subsidy programs to focus on small farmers and sustainable practices can promote a more equitable and environmentally friendly agricultural sector. Ensuring that support reaches those who truly need it fosters a healthier, more resilient food system.

Tech Regulation:

Overregulation of tech industries can stifle innovation and competitiveness. While regulations aim to protect consumers and ensure fair practices, excessive or poorly designed rules can hinder the growth of tech companies. This is especially true for startups that lack the resources to navigate complex regulatory landscapes. Encouraging a balanced approach to regulation can protect users while fostering an environment where innovation thrives. Policies that promote transparency, competition, and consumer rights without imposing undue burdens on businesses support a dynamic and forward-looking tech sector.

Homelessness:

Progressive policies tackling homelessness often resemble a game of whack-a-mole: hit one problem, and two more pop up elsewhere.

Progressive policies in cities often cannot address homelessness effectively. Despite significant spending on homelessness programs, many cities continue to see rising numbers of homeless individuals. Factors such as high housing costs, mental health issues, and substance abuse complicate the problem. Effective solutions require a comprehensive approach, including affordable housing initiatives, mental health services, and substance abuse treatment. Programs that focus solely on providing temporary shelter without addressing underlying causes tend to fall short. A holistic strategy that integrates housing, health, and social services can more effectively reduce homelessness.

Student Loans:

The cycle of rising tuition and easy loans is like throwing gasoline on a fire and then being surprised when things get out of control.

Federal student loan programs can contribute to rising tuition costs. Easy access to loans allows colleges to raise tuition without worrying about affordability for students. This creates a cycle where students take on more debt to pay higher prices, while institutions face little pressure to control costs. Reforming student loan programs to include accountability measures for colleges and promoting alternative funding models, such as income-share agreements, can help manage costs and reduce student debt burdens. Ensuring that higher education remains affordable and accessible is crucial for long-term economic growth.

Economic Mobility:

The U.S. still offers significant economic mobility compared to other countries. While income inequality often grabs headlines, the ability for individuals to move up the economic ladder is a critical measure of economic health. Policies that support education, job training, and entrepreneurship can enhance economic mobility, ensuring that people have the tools and opportunities to improve their circumstances. Addressing barriers to mobility, such as inadequate education or lack of access to capital, fosters a more inclusive and dynamic economy. Encouraging innovation and providing pathways for success supports a vibrant middle class and robust economic growth.

Climate Models:

Predicting climate with some models is like using a crystal ball—except the crystal ball is cracked and keeps changing its mind.

Climate models have often been inaccurate in their long-term predictions. While models are essential tools for understanding climate trends, their projections can vary widely based on assumptions and inputs. This uncertainty can lead to policy decisions that are overly cautious or insufficiently proactive. Improving the accuracy of climate models through better data collection and more sophisticated algorithms is crucial for effective policy-making. Transparent communication of the uncertainties and limitations of these models can help the public and policymakers make more informed decisions about climate action.

Deficit Spending:

Chronic deficit spending can lead to economic instability. When governments routinely spend more than they collect in revenue, they accumulate debt that can become unsustainable. This can lead to higher interest rates, inflation, and reduced investor confidence. Fiscal discipline, including balanced budgets and prudent spending, is essential to maintaining economic stability. Ensuring that government finances are managed responsibly helps avoid the negative consequences of excessive debt, such as economic downturns and reduced public services. Sustainable fiscal policies support long-term economic growth and stability.

Chronic deficit spending is like eating all your snacks in one go and wondering why you're starving the rest of the month.

1 - The Myth of Progressive Utopia

Why the Progressive Dream Fails

Progressive policies often present an alluring vision of a utopia where social justice, equality, and environmental sustainability reign supreme—kind of like a political Disneyland, minus the rides and with extra lines. However, the reality often falls short because of unrealistic assumptions and practical shortcomings. While the intentions behind these policies are noble, their implementation frequently leads to unintended consequences and systemic issues. After all, the road to hell is paved with good intentions and government paperwork.

One of the main pitfalls of progressive policies is the reliance on high taxes to fund expansive social programs. For instance, California, under Governor Gavin Newsom, has some of the highest taxes in the nation. Despite this, the state struggles with significant issues like homelessness, income inequality, and high living costs.

According to the Tax Foundation, California has the highest state income tax rate in the country, yet it ranks poorly in terms of business climate and economic freedom. High taxes can drive businesses and wealthy individuals out of the state, reducing the tax base and leading to budget shortfalls. It's amazing how quickly people can pack when there's a 13.3% state income tax waiting to greet them at home.

Over-regulation is another significant issue. Progressive areas often implement stringent regulations intended to protect the environment and ensure fair labor practices. While these regulations are well-meaning, they can stifle innovation and economic growth.

For example, New York City's economic policies under Mayor Bill de Blasio have included increased minimum wage laws and extensive rent control measures. It's almost like they believe you can legislate prosperity with a pen and a wish.

While these policies aim to help low-income workers and tenants, they have also led to higher unemployment rates among young and unskilled workers and a decrease in available rental properties. The New York City Rent Guidelines Board found that rent control can lead to housing shortages and reduced maintenance by landlords, ultimately harming the very people it aims to help.

Economic stagnation is a common consequence in heavily progressive areas. It's as if these regions are testing the theory that you can freeze an economy in bureaucratic amber. High taxes and over-regulation can deter investment and entrepreneurship, leading to slower economic growth.

A study by the American Legislative Exchange Council (ALEC) found that states with more progressive policies tend to have lower economic growth rates compared to those with more market-friendly policies. This stagnation can cause fewer job opportunities, lower wages, and a reduced quality of life for residents.

Progressive policies often underestimate the complexity of social issues. For example, efforts to defund the police in cities like Minneapolis have led to increased crime rates and longer response times for emergency services. It's almost as if taking cops off the streets makes it harder to catch criminals—who knew?

According to the Minneapolis Police Department's crime data, violent crime surged by 17% following cuts to the police budget in 2020. This highlights the practical shortcomings of well-intentioned policies that fail to consider the full spectrum of their impact.

Reputable sources and statistics back these observations. Because who doesn't trust statistics, especially when they support your point of view? The U.S. Census Bureau, Bureau of Economic Analysis, and various economic think tanks provide data illustrating the economic challenges faced by progressive regions.

For instance, California's high poverty rate, despite its wealth, is documented by the U.S. Census Bureau's Supplemental Poverty Measure. This measure takes into account the high cost of living and shows that California has one of the highest poverty rates in the nation.

In conclusion, while the progressive dream is built on admirable goals, its policies often falter because of high taxes, over-regulation, economic stagnation, and a failure to fully grasp the complexities of social issues. The experiences of states like California and cities like New York provide concrete examples of these shortcomings. By examining these cases and understanding the data, we can better appreciate why the progressive dream often remains just that—a dream.

Undeniable Facts

1. The Origin of the Term "Progressive"

The term "progressive" traces its roots back to the Progressive Era in the late 19th and early 20th centuries in the United States. This period was characterized by widespread social activism and political reform aimed at addressing issues such as corruption, monopolies, and social injustices. Progressives sought to improve society through government intervention, emphasizing the need for new policies and regulations to ensure fairness and equity.

2. Historical Examples of Failed Progressive Policies

- **Prohibition (1920-1933):** The 18th Amendment aimed to reduce crime and corruption by banning alcohol. Instead, it led to a rise in illegal speakeasies, bootlegging, and organized crime.

- **Great Society Programs (1960s)**: President Lyndon B. Johnson's ambitious social welfare programs aimed at eliminating poverty and racial injustice. While some aspects, like Medicare, have been successful, others have been criticized for creating dependency and failing to achieve their goals.
- **Rent Control Laws**: Implemented in various cities to keep housing affordable. These laws often lead to reduced investment in property maintenance and development, resulting in housing shortages and poor living conditions.

3. Notable Quotes from Prominent Progressives

- **Franklin D. Roosevelt**: "The only thing we have to fear is fear itself."
- **John F. Kennedy**: "Ask not what your country can do for you—ask what you can do for your country."
- **Bernie Sanders**: "For many, the American Dream has become a nightmare."
- **Elizabeth Warren**: "Balancing the budget on the backs of the poor is an exercise in cruelty."

4. Surprising Statistics About Economic Growth in Progressive vs. Conservative States

- **Job Growth**: According to the Bureau of Labor Statistics, from 2010 to 2020, Texas (a conservative state) experienced a job growth rate of 22%, compared with California's (a progressive state) 15%.
- **Business Climate**: The Tax Foundation's 2021 State Business Tax Climate Index ranks conservative states like Wyoming and South Dakota in the top 10, while progressive states like New York and California rank near the bottom.
- **Population Growth**: Census data shows conservative states like Florida and Texas have seen significant population increases. By comparison, states like New York and Illinois have experienced

population declines, reflecting economic opportunities and quality of life differences.

5. Unintended Consequences of Well-Intentioned Policies

- **Affordable Care Act (ACA)**: Aimed to provide health insurance for all, the ACA led to increased premiums and limited choices for some consumers, as insurers struggled with the new regulations.
- **Minimum Wage Increases**: Intended to raise living standards, significant hikes in the minimum wage have sometimes resulted in higher unemployment rates among young and unskilled workers, as businesses cut jobs or turn to automation.
- **Environmental Regulations**: Strict environmental laws, while protecting ecosystems, have sometimes stifled economic growth and innovation, particularly in industries like manufacturing and energy.
- **Social Welfare Programs**: Programs designed to support low-income families can create dependency, reducing the incentive to seek employment and self-sufficiency. For example, the welfare reforms of the 1990s sought to address this issue by encouraging work requirements.

The Psychological Toll of Progressive Policies

Living under progressive governance might seem like a dream to some, but for many, it's a source of significant emotional and mental strain. The constant push for higher taxes, more regulations, and the relentless pursuit of social justice can create a pressure cooker environment. This section explores how these policies affect the well-being of individuals.

Imagine living in a state where you feel like you're always one step away from a bureaucratic nightmare. High taxes and strict regulations can lead to constant financial stress. The guilt imposed by progressive narratives, which often suggest that individuals must bear the burden of societal issues, can further exacerbate mental strain. For example, residents in high-tax states like You have an email New Jersey often report higher levels of financial anxiety, constantly worrying about making ends meet while contributing to a seemingly bottomless pit of state expenditures.

Consider Oregon, where strict environmental and business regulations have created a challenging climate for small businesses. Business owners report feeling overwhelmed and stressed, trying to navigate a maze of regulations just to keep their doors open. Studies show that these regulatory pressures contribute to higher levels of anxiety and depression among entrepreneurs.

In New York, a state renowned for its progressive policies, residents often face high living costs and intense stress. A study from the American Psychological Association found that New Yorkers report some of the highest stress levels in the country, citing financial concerns and regulatory pressures as primary contributors.

Mental health data supports the notion that progressive policies can have detrimental effects on emotional well-being. Progressive states like California, New York, and New Jersey consistently report higher rates of mental health issues. The relentless drive for social change, while noble in intent, often leaves individuals feeling burned out and helpless. The stress of complying with ever-changing regulations and the guilt of not doing enough to support every cause can weigh heavily on residents.

In high-tax states like New Jersey, the financial burden can be overwhelming. Residents often joke that they need to consult their accountants more than their doctors. This constant financial juggling act contributes to chronic stress and anxiety.

In Oregon, small business owners feel like they're stuck in a never-ending episode of *"Survivor: Bureaucracy Edition."* The stress of adhering to stringent environmental regulations can lead to significant mental health issues, including anxiety and depression. Business owners report that the joy of entrepreneurship is often overshadowed by the fear of regulatory penalties.

To lighten this serious topic and make it a little easier to swallow, let's compare dealing with progressive policies to the stages of grief:

1. **Denial**: "There's no way they passed another tax increase. It must be a typo!"
2. **Anger**: "Why do I have to pay for everyone else's mistakes?!"
3. **Bargaining**: "If I recycle twice as much, can I get a tax break?"

4. **Depression**: "I'll never be able to afford my dream home with these property taxes."
5. **Acceptance**: "Well, at least the potholes might get fixed... eventually."

2 - Understanding Liberal Ideology

The Science of Liberal Thinking

In this chapter, we'll explore the psychology behind liberal thinking, breaking it down into digestible bits. Imagine liberal ideology as a lazy office worker who, despite all the fancy tools at their disposal, still manages to bungle the simplest tasks now and then. This is our metaphorical guide through the intricate maze of the liberal mind.

Psychological and Sociological Basis of Liberal Ideology

Liberal thinking often stems from a combination of cognitive and emotional traits that shape decision-making processes. To understand this, we need to dive into the world of moral psychology and political ideology, particularly the work of scholars like Jonathan Haidt.

1. **Cognitive Dissonance**: Liberals often find themselves in the throes of cognitive dissonance, a mental tug-of-war that creates a palpable sense of discomfort. Imagine the sensation of trying to hold two opposing magnets together—the repelling force mirrors the tension in their minds.

This dissonance emerges when they support free speech but also push for restrictions to prevent hate speech. It's like walking a tightrope, balancing precariously between the ideals of open dialogue and the fear of harmful rhetoric. This mental gymnastics not only strains their logic but also leads to policies that feel as inconsistent as a wobbly table with mismatched legs. The contradictions are as jarring as a sudden cold draft in a warm room, unsettling and difficult to reconcile.

1. **Emotional Reasoning**: Liberals often prioritize emotional reasoning, crafting decisions based more on feelings than on hard empirical evidence. Picture this: a lazy office worker nestled comfortably in their plush chair, choosing to savor the warmth of their seat rather than venturing out to gather the cold, hard facts from a report. This

comfort-seeking behavior parallels the liberal tendency to lean on emotional appeals.

In the political arena, these emotional narratives are like a cozy blanket, wrapping supporters in a sense of compassion and righteousness. However, this emotional warmth often casts a shadow over logical arguments, much like a fireplace's glow obscures the flicker of a distant candle. Policies born from this mindset are driven by feelings, offering the immediate comfort of a heated room but lacking the practicality needed for lasting solutions. The result is a political approach that, while heartwarming, can often be as impractical as trying to write a report while wrapped in a snug, sleep-inducing blanket.

Research on Cognitive and Emotional Traits

Jonathan Haidt's studies on moral psychology provide valuable insights into the liberal mindset. He identifies several moral foundations that underpin liberal ideology:

- **Care/Harm**: Liberals heavily emphasize care and compassion, often advocating for policies that protect the vulnerable. This is why welfare programs, healthcare reforms, and environmental regulations are central to liberal agendas.
- **Fairness/Cheating**: The liberal focus on fairness leads to support for progressive taxation and social justice initiatives. However, this can sometimes result in policies that prioritize equality over efficiency, much like our office worker spending more time organizing their desk than actually working.

Specific Examples and Studies

Let's look at some concrete examples to illustrate these concepts:

1. **Cognitive Dissonance**: A study by Stanford University found that liberals often grapple with the delicate balance between upholding free speech and preventing harm. This struggle creates a complex

dance between two conflicting ideals. On one hand, liberals champion open dialogue, advocating for a society where diverse voices and opinions can be heard. This is akin to a bustling marketplace of ideas, vibrant and full of life, where debate and discussion thrive.

On the other hand, they also endorse restrictions aimed at preventing offensive or harmful speech. This protective instinct is like a gardener carefully pruning a rose bush, trying to remove only the thorns while preserving the beauty of the flowers. However, this task is far from simple. The dual commitment to free expression and harm prevention often results in policies that seem contradictory, much like a painting with clashing colors that struggle to form a coherent image.

Imagine a university as a circus ring where the ringmaster encourages wild, daring performances but suddenly steps in to stop any act that seems too dangerous or offensive. The performers, confused, juggle their freedom with fear of being yanked off stage. It's a bit like trying to follow a road map with conflicting directions—one path leading towards unrestrained freedom and the other towards cautious regulation.

These policies, while well-intentioned, can inadvertently stifle the very dialogue they aim to protect. By seeking to shield individuals from harm, they risk creating echo chambers where only certain viewpoints are safe to express. Picture this: a comedy club where every joke needs to pass through a sensitivity committee. The result? Comedians are left trying to be funny without offending anyone, leading to routines that are as bland as unseasoned tofu.

The result is a landscape where the ideals of free speech and protection from harm coexist uneasily, leading to an ongoing debate about the best way to balance these critical values. So, next time you hear a policy that sounds like it's trying to be both a strict librarian and a free-spirited poet, remember: it's just the latest act in the liberal circus.

1. **Emotional Reasoning**: Research from Yale University shows that emotional appeals in political campaigns are particularly effective among liberal voters. Imagine a political rally where the air is thick with sentimentality, and the crowd sways like a field of wheat in a gentle breeze, moved by stories of empathy and compassion. Campaigns that highlight these values tend to resonate deeply, pulling at heartstrings and influencing voting behavior in ways that hard data and statistics simply cannot.

It's as if liberal voters have a built-in radar for emotional narratives, detecting them as easily as the scent of freshly baked cookies wafting through the air. The speeches are filled with vivid imagery and heartfelt anecdotes, painting pictures so moving that even the most stoic attendees find themselves misty-eyed. Picture a candidate recounting the tale of a struggling single mother who overcame adversity thanks to community support—an appeal that hits home harder than a sledgehammer to a piñata.

In contrast, attempts to win over these voters with dry policy details and economic forecasts fall flatter than a pancake on a Sunday morning. It's like trying to sell ice cream with a spreadsheet instead of a scoop—utterly unappealing. The emotional narratives act as a warm embrace, making voters feel connected and understood, much like a cozy blanket on a chilly night.

Campaigns savvy to this dynamic craft their messages like master chefs, blending empathy and compassion into a rich, irresistible stew that leaves voters hungry for more. This culinary approach to politics can be humorously compared to a cook-off, where the dish with the most heartwarming story behind it wins, regardless of its actual taste.

So, when you see a political ad that feels like a Hallmark movie, complete with swelling music and tear-jerking moments, know that it's designed to tap into the emotional core of liberal voters. It's a strategy that turns every campaign event into a sensory experience, leaving a lasting impression that's as comforting as a favorite childhood memory.

1. **Jonathan Haidt's Work**: In his book *The Righteous Mind*, Haidt discusses how liberals prioritize care and fairness, sometimes at the expense of other moral values like loyalty and authority. This focus can lead to policies that, while well-intentioned, might overlook practical considerations.

In summary, liberal ideology is deeply rooted in psychological and sociological factors. Cognitive dissonance and emotional reasoning play significant roles in shaping liberal policies, often leading to a blend of compassionate intentions and impractical outcomes. Just like our lazy office worker, liberal thinking can sometimes be more about feeling good than getting the job done efficiently.

By understanding these underlying factors, we can better navigate the political landscape and make more informed decisions. So, next time you encounter a liberal policy, remember the lazy office worker—it might just help you see things a little more clearly.

The Evolution and Impact of Liberal Ideology
Undeniable Facts:

1. **Historical Evolution of Liberal Thought** Liberal ideology has a rich history, evolving significantly over the centuries. Initially rooted in the Enlightenment era, liberal thought emphasized individual liberty, reason, and skepticism of authority. Over time, it transformed, incorporating social justice and economic equality into its core principles. Imagine the journey of liberal thought as a grand historical tapestry, each thread representing milestones like the American and French Revolutions, which championed liberty and democratic governance. This tapestry continues to evolve, weaving in

contemporary issues like climate change and digital privacy.

2. **Famous Liberal Thinkers and Their Contributions** Throughout history, numerous thinkers have shaped liberal ideology. John Locke, often regarded as the father of liberalism, introduced ideas of natural rights and government by consent. John Stuart Mill expanded these concepts, advocating for individual freedom and utilitarianism. Fast forward to the 20th century, John Rawls introduced theories of justice as fairness, influencing modern liberal thought. Picture these intellectuals as trailblazers, illuminating paths of liberty and equality with their groundbreaking ideas.

3. **Surprising Psychological Traits Associated with Liberalism** Studies reveal intriguing psychological traits commonly found among liberals. They score higher on openness to experience, embracing novelty and change. Liberals also show greater sensitivity to perceived injustices, which fuels their passion for social equality and reform. Imagine a liberal mind as an adventurous explorer, always seeking new experiences and advocating for fairness in every corner of the world. This openness can sometimes lead to cognitive dissonance, where holding conflicting beliefs creates mental discomfort, much like trying to mix oil and water.

4. **Notable Liberal Policies and Their Sociological Impacts** Various liberal policies have left lasting marks on society. Welfare programs, aimed at reducing poverty and inequality, have provided crucial support to millions. Environmental regulations strive to protect our planet for future generations. However, these policies often come with unintended consequences. For instance, generous welfare programs can sometimes create dependency, while stringent environmental laws might stifle economic growth. Visualize these policies as double-edged swords, capable of both significant benefits and unforeseen drawbacks.

5. **Quotes from Influential Liberal Philosophers.**
   - John Locke: "All mankind... being all equal and independent, no one ought to harm another in his life, health, liberty, or possessions."
   - John Stuart Mill: "The only freedom which deserves the

name is that of pursuing our own good in our own way."
- ○ John Rawls: "Justice is the first virtue of social institutions, as truth is of systems of thought."

These quotes encapsulate the essence of liberal philosophy, emphasizing individual rights, freedom, and justice. Imagine these words as guiding stars, illuminating the path for those who seek a society rooted in liberty and equality.

By understanding the historical context, influential thinkers, psychological traits, and real-world impacts of liberal policies, we gain a comprehensive view of liberal ideology. This knowledge empowers us to navigate the complex landscape of political beliefs with greater clarity and confidence.

The Role of Identity Politics

In the vibrant tapestry of liberal ideology, identity politics stands out like a cluster of mischievous gremlins, creating chaos and excitement. These gremlins, while aiming to ensure representation and equality, often end up causing more turmoil than harmony. Let's delve into how these gremlins influence liberal policies and societal dynamics, sprinkling a bit of humor and satire along the way.

Identity politics focuses on the interests and perspectives of social groups with which people identify. Picture a colorful parade where each group waves its unique flag, demanding attention and representation. This parade is a central feature of liberal thought, influencing policies designed to address historical injustices and systemic inequalities.

For example, affirmative action policies aim to level the playing field by giving underrepresented groups better access to education and employment. These policies, while well-intentioned, sometimes lead to accusations of reverse discrimination, creating a tug-of-war scenario where the gremlins tug on both ends of the rope, leaving everyone in a dizzying spin.

Identity politics can profoundly impact policy outcomes, sometimes in unexpected ways. Consider the controversy surrounding intersectionality, a concept that examines how various forms of discrimination intersect and compound. It's like the gremlins have discovered a magical mirror, reflecting multiple dimensions of identity, and are now throwing confetti everywhere, making it difficult to see the original issue clearly.

Take affirmative action as an example. While it seeks to address racial and gender disparities, it can inadvertently fuel resentment among those who feel they are unfairly disadvantaged by such measures. Imagine a college admissions office besieged by gremlins, each demanding special consideration based on a myriad of intersecting identities, leading to a chaotic, contentious environment.

The gremlins of identity politics often leave a trail of unintended consequences and social divisions in their wake. Policies meant to foster inclusivity can sometimes deepen societal rifts, as groups vie for recognition and resources. It's as if the gremlins have thrown a wild party, where everyone is invited but no one had fun.

For instance, while affirmative action aims to promote diversity, it can also lead to significant backlash and increased polarization. Data shows that political polarization has surged in recent years, with identity politics playing a crucial role. The gremlins seem to be at it again, setting up barriers and causing friction where unity was intended.

Research indicates that identity politics contributes to heightened political polarization. It's like the gremlins have divided the room into cliques, each suspicious of the other. A study by the Pew Research Center highlights that partisan antipathy has reached record levels, with individuals identifying more strongly with their social groups than ever before.

Consider the debates over gender-neutral bathrooms or the push for diverse representation in media. While these initiatives aim to foster inclusivity, they often spark heated debates and further entrench opposing viewpoints. The gremlins, it seems, have found a new playground, where every swing of the ideological pendulum sends sparks flying.

One prominent example is the affirmative action debate. Intended to rectify historical injustices, it has instead become a battleground. Universities implementing these policies are like arenas where the gremlins pit applicants against each other based on race and ethnicity, rather than merit alone.

Similarly, the concept of intersectionality, while academically significant, can lead to policy paralysis. When lawmakers try to address the needs of every intersecting identity, the result can be a tangled web of regulations that satisfy no one. It's as if the gremlins have spun a web so intricate that even they are stuck in it.

In summary, identity politics, much like our mischievous gremlins, plays a significant role in shaping liberal policies and societal dynamics. While aiming for equality and representation, these policies often lead to unintended consequences and increased polarization. Understanding this dynamic is crucial for navigating the complex landscape of modern politics, where every step forward can feel like a dance with gremlins, always on the brink of chaos and excitement.

HOW TO UNDERSTAND LEFT-WING POLITICAL SPIN

Undeniable Facts

1. **Key Moments in the History of Identity Politics:** Identity politics has shaped significant historical events and movements. One key moment was the Civil Rights Movement of the 1960s, which highlighted the struggle for racial equality and justice in the United States. Another pivotal moment was the rise of the feminist movement in the 1970s, advocating for women's rights and gender equality. More recently, the LGBTQ+ rights movement has gained prominence, challenging societal norms and pushing for legal recognition and protection. Each of these movements, driven by the needs and voices of marginalized groups, has left an indelible mark on society.

2. **Surprising Facts about the Origins of Identity Politics:** The term "identity politics" first gained traction in the 1970s, but its roots can be traced back to earlier social justice efforts. One surprising origin is the Combahee River Collective, a Black feminist lesbian organization formed in 1974. They issued a statement emphasizing the importance of addressing the interlocking oppressions of race, gender, and sexuality, laying the groundwork for what we now understand as intersectionality. This concept has since become a cornerstone of identity politics, highlighting how different aspects of identity intersect to shape individual experiences of oppression.

3. **Notable Identity Politics Movements and Their Impacts:** Several notable movements have emerged under the banner of identity politics, each bringing significant social change. The Black Lives Matter movement, for example, has brought international attention to issues of police brutality and systemic racism. The #MeToo movement has shed light on sexual harassment and assault, empowering survivors to speak out. These movements, while sometimes controversial, have spurred important conversations and policy changes, demonstrating the power of collective identity in driving societal progress.

4. **Quotes from Both Supporters and Critics of Identity Politics**
   - **Supporters**:
     - Kimberlé Crenshaw: "Intersectionality is a lens through which you can see where power comes and collides, where it interlocks and intersects."
     - Audre Lorde: "There is no thing as a single-issue struggle because we do not live single-issue lives."
   - **Critics**:
     - Mark Lilla: "Identity politics on the left was at first about large classes of people—African-Americans, women, gays—seeking to redress major historical wrongs by mobilizing and then working through our political institutions to secure their rights."
     - Jordan Peterson: "The idea that you can target an ethnic group with a collective crime, regardless of the specific innocence or guilt of the constituent elements of that group, there is nothing that's more racist than that."

5. **Interesting Data on the Demographics of Identity Politics:** Demographic data reveals intriguing insights into the support base of identity politics. Studies show that younger generations, particularly millennials and Gen Z, are more likely to engage in and support identity politics. This trend is reflected in the increasing diversity of political activism and advocacy groups. Additionally, women and racial minorities are more likely to prioritize issues related to identity politics, such as gender equality and racial justice. Data from the Pew Research Center indicates that these groups view identity-based movements as essential to achieving social justice and equality.

3 - Big Government: The Liberal Answer to Everything

Spending More Money on Problems

Liberal policies often approach societal problems with a simple solution: throw money at them. This default strategy leads to inefficiencies and unintended consequences, much like giving a shopaholic an unlimited credit card—it's exhilarating initially but devastating when the bill arrives.

Liberal spending habits can create significant inefficiencies. The idea is that more money will fix issues like education, healthcare, and poverty. However, increased spending doesn't always mean better outcomes. For instance, in states like California and New York, high social welfare spending hasn't led to improved living conditions.

In California, Proposition 13, passed in 1978, aimed to limit property taxes. While it was meant to keep housing affordable, it also slashed local government revenue, leading to increased reliance on state funds for schools and public services. The state then boosted spending to cover the shortfall, but the quality of education and public services didn't improve proportionately. Schools struggled with overcrowding, teacher shortages, and outdated materials despite the influx of state funds.

Under Governor Andrew Cuomo, New York's budget policies focused on high spending to support extensive social programs. Despite this, the state consistently faced budget deficits and growing debt. For example, in 2020, New York's budget deficit soared to $6.1 billion, forcing the state to cut funding for essential services despite high overall spending. The state invested heavily in Medicaid, yet many hospitals remained under-funded and understaffed, struggling to meet the needs of their communities.

According to the Congressional Budget Office, excessive government spending can lead to large budget deficits and increased national debt, which, in turn, can stifle economic growth. When states like California and New York prioritize spending over balanced budgets, they often experience economic challenges. This mismanagement isn't just a theoretical issue—it's a practical one affecting millions of residents.

In Illinois, the state's pension crisis serves as another example of liberal spending gone awry. Illinois has one of the highest pension debts in the nation, with unfunded liabilities exceeding $137 billion. Despite high taxes and significant contributions to pension funds, the financial health of Illinois remains precarious, leading to cuts in essential services and infrastructure projects.

Detroit's bankruptcy in 2013 is a stark reminder of what happens when spending spirals out of control. The city's liberal policies led to extensive social programs and infrastructure projects that were not sustainable long-term. The result was an $18 billion debt, the largest municipal bankruptcy in U.S. history. Detroit's experience illustrates that without proper financial management, generous spending can lead to economic collapse.

Throwing more money at problems is a shortsighted error in judgment. Liberal policies often fail to consider the long-term consequences and the importance of efficient spending. Instead of addressing the root causes of issues, they apply a temporary, costly band-aid. This approach not only wastes resources but also perpetuates the problems it aims to solve, ultimately hurting the very people it intends to help.

Imagine the government is a teenager with a credit card that has no limit. The first few shopping sprees are exhilarating—new gadgets, fancy clothes, all the latest trends. But then, the bill arrives. Suddenly, that limitless card doesn't seem like such a great idea. The government's approach to spending often mirrors this scenario: fun and games until reality hits.

While liberal policies advocate for increased spending to solve societal issues, this approach often leads to inefficiencies and unintended consequences. The examples of California and New York illustrate that more money doesn't always mean better outcomes, and the long-term economic impact can be significant. So, next time you hear about a new government spending initiative, remember: it might be fun at first, but eventually, the bill comes due.

Undeniable Facts

1. **Historical examples of excessive government spending**: The New Deal in the 1930s, initiated by President Franklin D. Roosevelt, significantly increased federal spending and debt through programs like Social Security and public works projects. While it aimed to alleviate the Great Depression, it also set a precedent for large-scale government intervention in the economy.

2. **Famous budget crises in liberal states**: California faced a severe budget crisis in 2009, with a $26 billion deficit leading to drastic cuts in education and social services. This crisis highlighted the state's struggle to balance generous social spending with fiscal responsibility.

3. **Notable quotes about government spending**: Ronald Reagan famously said, "Government's view of the economy could be summed up in a few short phrases: If it moves, tax it. If it keeps moving, regulate it. And if it stops moving, subsidize it." This quote reflects the skepticism towards government intervention and spending.

4. **Fun facts about the national debt**: As of 2021, the U.S. national debt exceeded $28 trillion, more than the country's GDP. This staggering figure underscores the long-term fiscal challenges facing the nation due to continuous deficit spending.

5. **Surprising economic impacts of liberal spending policies**: Excessive spending can lead to inflation, reduced private sector investment, and slower economic growth. For example, the post-2008 financial crisis stimulus efforts, while necessary for recovery, also contributed to long-term debt and economic instability.

6. **Key legislative bills associated with increased spending**: The Affordable Care Act (2010), also known as Obamacare, expanded healthcare spending significantly by providing subsidies and expanding Medicaid. This legislation aimed to reduce the number of uninsured Americans but also increased federal and state healthcare expenditures.

7. **Dates and outcomes of major spending initiatives**: The American Recovery and Reinvestment Act of 2009 aimed to stimulate the economy post-recession with a $787 billion package. While it helped prevent a deeper recession, it also added significantly to the national debt and sparked debates over the effectiveness of large-scale stimulus spending.

8. **Notable politicians known for high spending policies**: Bernie Sanders, a prominent progressive, advocates for expansive government programs such as Medicare for All and free college tuition. These proposals would require substantial increases in federal spending and taxation.

9. **Comparisons of spending between liberal and conservative states**: Liberal states like California and New York often have higher per capita spending compared to conservative states like Texas and

Florida. For instance, California's per capita spending is approximately $12,000, while Texas spends around $8,000 per capita, reflecting different priorities in budget allocations.

10. **Case studies of specific programs with excessive budgets**: The California High-Speed Rail project, initially estimated at $33 billion, ballooned to $100 billion and remains incomplete. This project has been criticized for its cost overruns and delays, illustrating the challenges of managing large-scale public infrastructure projects.

The Inefficiency and Inequity of Forced Equality

Policies aimed at forced equality often lead to inefficiencies and unintended inequities, creating more problems than they solve. These policies, while well-intentioned, can distort markets and individual incentives, leading to outcomes that are neither fair nor efficient. Frankly, you'd have to be thick in the head, know nothing about finances or basic math, or suffer from severe liberalism (don't worry, it's curable) to think that repeating these same types of policies over and over will produce more productive results.

Liberal policies that mandate equality can disrupt natural economic and social dynamics. They can create a false sense of achievement and undermine meritocracy. For example, affirmative action, wealth redistribution programs, and minimum wage laws aim to level the playing field but often result in unintended negative consequences.

Affirmative action in college admissions aims to increase diversity by giving preferential treatment to underrepresented groups. However, this can lead to reverse discrimination, where more qualified candidates are overlooked because of their race or ethnicity. Studies show that affirmative action can also set up students for failure by placing them in academic environments where they are underprepared, leading to higher dropout rates. For example, a study by the University of California found that ending affirmative action in college admissions led to improved graduation rates for minority students, suggesting that students perform better in environments that match their academic preparation.

Wealth redistribution efforts, such as those under President Lyndon B. Johnson's Great Society programs, aimed to reduce poverty through extensive social welfare initiatives. While these programs helped some, they also created dependency and disincentives to work. The U.S. Census Bureau reports that despite trillions of dollars spent on these programs, the poverty rate has remained relatively unchanged since the 1960s. This stagnation indicates that simply transferring wealth doesn't address the root causes of poverty or promote self-sufficiency. Despite the good intentions, the long-term economic impacts have been less than stellar, showing that throwing money at the problem doesn't always yield results.

Minimum wage laws are intended to ensure a living wage for all workers. However, they can lead to higher unemployment rates, particularly among low-skilled workers. Businesses facing higher labor costs may reduce hiring, cut hours, or increase automation, which disproportionately affects the very people the laws are meant to help. A 2019 study by the Congressional Budget Office found that increasing the federal minimum wage to $15 an hour could result in 1.3 million job losses, highlighting the trade-offs between higher wages and employment opportunities. It's an unfortunate reality that policies designed to help workers can sometimes end up hurting them the most.

It doesn't take a genius (like me) to figure out that the costs of these wage increases are always passed along to the consumer. *They have to!* There's no way to avoid it. Companies can't simply change their entire financial structure, simultaneously reducing their bottom lines. The whole point to being in business is to make money.

So the first thing that happens when you have to pay your employees more is the frustrating task of releasing the ones you can't afford. And you're back to Square One. Some people make a little more. Others are added back into the ranks of the unemployed, where many will have to rely on government assistance and—well, you get the idea. The entire vicious cycle is a never-ending exercise in futility.

Or, if you suffer from a bad case of liberalism, an exercise in the "greatest thing we can do for our fellow Americans. It's the right thing to do. With or without bi-partisan support, we must pass laws to pay people more!"

sigh

Not surprisingly, even with the aforementioned knowledge, most states have implemented the minimum wage increase anyhow. Sure, go ahead. Enjoy the temporary euphoria of pleasing the smallest segment of society. And then look the other way when the after-affects kick in for the rest of the population.

Economic studies, such as those conducted by the National Bureau of Economic Research, indicate that forced equality policies often fail to achieve their goals. For instance, affirmative action can result in mismatched placements, wealth redistribution can stagnate social mobility, and minimum wage increases can lead to job losses. These outcomes suggest that the liberal approach to forced equality often backfires, creating more challenges than it resolves.

Specific Examples

- **Affirmative Action**: A study by the University of California found that ending affirmative action in college admissions led to improved graduation rates for minority students, suggesting that students perform better in environments that match their academic preparation.
- **Wealth Redistribution**: President Johnson's Great Society programs aimed to eliminate poverty and racial injustice. Despite significant investment, poverty rates have not significantly declined, pointing to inefficiencies in how resources are allocated.
- **Minimum Wage Laws**: A 2019 study by the Congressional Budget Office found that increasing the federal minimum wage to $15 an hour could result in 1.3 million job losses, highlighting the trade-offs between higher wages and employment opportunities.

The Gold Star Analogy

Forced equality is like giving everyone a gold star, regardless of effort. Imagine a classroom where every student, no matter how hard they work or how much they slack off, receives the same grade. The result? The hardworking students feel demotivated, and the slackers have no incentive to improve. It's a recipe for mediocrity, not excellence.

While liberal policies aimed at forced equality strive for fairness, they often lead to inefficiencies and unintended inequities. By distorting incentives and market dynamics, these policies can do more harm than good, ultimately hurting the very individuals they intend to help.

Undeniable Facts

Historical examples of forced equality: Mao Zedong's Great Leap Forward in China aimed to transform the country into a socialist society through rapid industrialization and collectivization. The policies resulted in widespread famine and the deaths of an estimated 15 to 45 million people, highlighting the disastrous consequences of forced equality.

Notable failures of egalitarian policies: The Kibbutz movement in Israel, which aimed to create a communal society where resources and profits were shared equally, has largely declined. Many kibbutzim faced financial difficulties and had to abandon their egalitarian principles, transitioning to more market-oriented approaches.

Quotes about the dangers of forced equality: Margaret Thatcher remarked, "The problem with socialism is that you eventually run out of other people's money." This quote underscores the unsustainable nature of forced wealth redistribution.

Interesting statistics on inequality in different political contexts: A study by the Brookings Institution found that income inequality has grown faster in cities with more progressive policies compared to those with conservative governance. This challenges the effectiveness of liberal policies in reducing economic disparities.

Fun facts about social mobility: Research from the Equality of Opportunity Project shows that children from low-income families in Salt Lake City, a more conservative city, have higher rates of upward mobility compared to those in San Francisco, a liberal city, indicating that conservative policies may foster better opportunities for economic advancement.

Key legislative bills aimed at forced equality: The Dodd-Frank Wall Street Reform and Consumer Protection Act of 2010 intended to increase financial stability and protect consumers but has faced criticism for creating regulatory burdens that disproportionately affect smaller banks and financial institutions.

Dates and outcomes of major equality initiatives: The Equal Pay Act of 1963 aimed to abolish wage disparity based on sex. While it has had some success, studies indicate that the gender pay gap persists, suggesting that legislation alone cannot achieve complete equality.

Notable politicians known for promoting forced equality: Elizabeth Warren has championed policies like wealth taxes and student loan forgiveness, advocating for significant government intervention to address economic disparities. Her proposals often spark debates on their feasibility and economic impact.

Comparisons of equality policies between liberal and conservative states: States like New Hampshire, which has no state income tax and lower social welfare spending, often report better economic performance and lower unemployment rates compared to high-tax, high-spending states like Connecticut.

Case studies of specific forced equality programs and their results: The UK's National Health Service (NHS), established to provide healthcare for all, faces chronic underfunding and long wait times for patients. While the NHS ensures access to healthcare, it also struggles with inefficiencies and resource allocation, illustrating the complexities of implementing forced equality in public services.

4 – The Social Fabric Unraveled

The Unintended Consequences of Good Intentions

In this enlightening exposé, let's dig into the tangled mess that is the housing crisis and homelessness in our liberal strongholds. Spoiler alert: it's not as simple as blaming capitalism or bad luck.

Nope, we're diving into the nitty-gritty of policies that were supposed to help, but somehow managed to make things worse. Think of it as a game of musical chairs—except someone forgot to add enough chairs, and now everyone's left standing, scratching their heads.

A Perfect Storm of Policies

Liberal policies are often rooted in good intentions. However, we all know the road to housing hell is paved with them. Take rent control, for example. The idea is to keep housing affordable, but what happens when landlords can't make a profit? They stop investing in their properties, and voilà, you have a shortage of decent places to live. Let's look at the numbers: In San Francisco, a city with some of the strictest rent control laws, the average rent for a one-bedroom apartment is still over $3,000 a month. Affordable? Not so much.

Zoning laws are another culprit. In theory, they're there to maintain the character of neighborhoods. In practice, they often prevent the construction of new housing, leading to a scarcity that drives up prices. Seattle is a prime example. The city's strict zoning laws have kept housing supply low, even as demand has skyrocketed. The result? A booming homeless population that the city just can't seem to get a handle on.

And let's not forget high taxes. They're supposed to fund public services, but in reality, they often drive out businesses and residents. Take a look at Los Angeles, where high taxes have coincided with a spike in homelessness. The city has implemented countless measures to tackle the problem, yet the numbers continue to rise. As of the last count, there were over 41,000 homeless people in LA County.

Read that again!

Not in one state.

In one county! 41,000 and growing! It's unthinkable! And inexcusable.

Case Studies: Proposition 10 and New York's Rent Control

Let's get specific. California's Proposition 10 aimed to expand rent control, but studies showed it would likely lead to a reduction in rental housing supply, worsening the crisis. Thankfully, voters saw the light and rejected it. The fact that it made the ballot reveals the misguidedness of certain policy proposals.

Meanwhile, in New York, decades of rent control laws have created a bifurcated market where long-term tenants enjoy artificially low rents, while newcomers face exorbitant prices. The market distortion has led to disinvestment in rental properties, contributing to a housing stock that is old and in disrepair.

The Data Doesn't Lie

According to the U.S. Department of Housing and Urban Development (HUD), cities with stringent housing regulations and high taxes tend to have higher rates of homelessness. HUD's 2023 Annual Homeless Assessment Report reveals that on a single night in January 2023, over 650,000 people were experiencing homelessness, a 12% increase from 2022. This marks the highest number since reporting began in 2007. The rise in homelessness is largely due to a sharp increase in first-time homelessness, with the number of newly homeless individuals jumping by 25% between 2021 and 2022.

Liberal policies in California, like rent control and zoning laws, have unintended consequences of driving out landlords and hindering new housing projects. San Francisco, Los Angeles, and Seattle are prime examples where these policies have led to severe housing shortages and skyrocketing rents. The average rent for a one-bedroom apartment in San Francisco is still over $3,000, despite the city's stringent rent control measures.

HUD's data paints a grim picture: between 2022 and 2023, the number of unsheltered homeless individuals increased by 23,000 people, or 11%. Even more startling, the number of families experiencing homelessness saw a 16% rise, reversing a decade-long trend of decline.

The Biden Administration's American Rescue Plan (ARP) initially helped prevent a rise in homelessness during the pandemic, but as these resources expired, the numbers surged again. Rental housing conditions have been extraordinarily challenging, with rents increasing by over 9% between 2021 and 2022, exacerbating the crisis.

So, the numbers don't lie: the well-intentioned policies meant to protect renters and maintain neighborhood integrity often end up exacerbating the very problems they aim to solve. It's like a game of musical chairs—except someone forgot to add enough chairs, and now everyone's left standing, wondering what went wrong.

Wrapping Up the Musical Chairs Game

So, what's the takeaway here? Liberal policies, despite their well-meaning origins, often unravel the social fabric they're meant to strengthen. By understanding the real-world impacts of rent control, zoning laws, and high taxes, we can start to see through the political spin and develop more effective solutions.

Remember, with housing, we all need a seat. And if there aren't enough to go around, it's time to rethink how we're playing the game.

Undeniable Facts

1. **Notable spikes in homelessness:**

- ◦ **2023:** Homelessness surged by 12% from 2022, with over 650,000 people experiencing homelessness on a single night in January 2023, the highest number since 2007.
- ◦ **2008 Financial Crisis:** Homelessness saw significant increases across the U.S., driven by widespread foreclosures and job losses.

2. **Historical attempts to solve housing crises:**
   - ◦ **New Deal Era (1930s):** The Public Works Administration (PWA) and later the Federal Housing Administration (FHA) were created to address housing shortages during the Great Depression.
   - ◦ **Post-WWII:** The GI Bill helped returning veterans purchase homes, leading to the suburban housing boom.

3. **Famous quotes about housing policies:**
   - ◦ "A house is made of walls and beams; a home is built with love and dreams." - Unknown
   - ◦ "Housing is absolutely essential to human flourishing. Without stable shelter, it all falls apart." - Matthew Desmond

4. **Surprising statistics on housing affordability:**
   - ◦ As of 2023, over 11 million renter households spend over 50% of their income on housing.
   - ◦ The average rent for a one-bedroom apartment in San Francisco is over $3,000.

5. **Fun facts about housing markets in different states:**
   - ◦ **Texas:** Known for its affordable housing, the median home price in Texas is significantly lower than in states like California and New York.
   - ◦ **Florida:** Despite being a popular destination for retirees, Florida has seen a rapid increase in housing costs due to high demand.

6. **Key legislative bills related to housing and homelessness:**
   - ◦ **McKinney-Vento Homeless Assistance Act (1987):** The first major federal legislative response to homelessness,

providing federal funds for shelter programs.
- **California's Proposition 10 (2018):** Proposed to expand rent control, but was rejected by voters due to concerns it would worsen the housing shortage.

7. **Dates and outcomes of major housing initiatives:**
   - **1949:** The Housing Act of 1949 aimed to provide "a decent home and a suitable living environment for every American family," leading to urban renewal projects.
   - **2021-2022:** The American Rescue Plan included significant funding to prevent and address homelessness, temporarily stabilizing numbers before they surged again in 2023.

8. **Notable politicians involved in housing policies:**
   - **Franklin D. Roosevelt:** Pushed for New Deal housing programs.
   - **Barack Obama:** Advocated for affordable housing and implemented the Housing and Economic Recovery Act.
   - **Gavin Newsom:** Current Governor of California, known for his ambitious (yet controversial) housing policies.

9. **Comparisons of homelessness rates between liberal and conservative cities:**
   - Liberal cities like San Francisco, Los Angeles, and Seattle have some of the highest homelessness rates due to stringent housing regulations and high living costs.
   - Conservative cities like Dallas and Phoenix have lower homelessness rates, partly due to less restrictive housing policies and lower living costs.

10. **Case studies of specific housing policies and their impacts:**
    - **Rent Control in New York:** Long-term rent control has led to a bifurcated market, where long-time renters pay low rents while new renters face high prices, reducing incentives for landlords to maintain properties.
    - **Houston's Housing First Approach:** Focuses on providing permanent housing to homeless individuals without preconditions, which has shown success in reducing

homelessness.

The Decline of Public Education
The Education System: A Sinking Ship

Imagine public education as a massive ship. Everyone's scrambling to patch the holes, but no matter how hard they try, the water keeps rushing in. That's the state of our public schools today, largely due to liberal policies that, despite their good intentions, have caused more harm than good.

The Impact of Liberal Policies on Public Education

Liberal policies have led to declining standards and poor performance in public schools. For starters, let's talk about **teacher unions**. While unions are supposed to protect teachers' rights, they often end up prioritizing job security over educational quality.

The result? Incompetent teachers remain in the system, and innovative reforms are blocked. For example, in Chicago, one of the largest public school systems in the country, teacher strikes have repeatedly disrupted education, and the performance metrics are nothing to boast about. According to the National Center for Education Statistics (NCES), Chicago public schools have graduation rates below the national average and test scores that lag significantly

.

Funding Disparities and Mismanagement

Funding disparities are another critical issue. Liberal policies often advocate for increased funding without addressing how that money is spent. The result is a mismanagement of resources, where administrative costs balloon while classrooms remain under-funded. In Detroit, for instance, the public school system received millions in federal aid, yet schools continue to struggle with basic infrastructure problems, such as heating failures and outdated textbooks . The NCES reports that, despite receiving substantial funding, Detroit public schools have some of the lowest test scores in the nation.

Curriculum Changes and Performance

Then there's the issue of curriculum changes. The introduction of the Common Core standards was intended to provide a consistent, clear understanding of what students are expected to learn. However, it has faced significant backlash for being too rigid and not accommodating diverse learning styles. The implementation has been patchy at best, leading to confusion among teachers and students alike. Washington D.C. public schools, for example, have struggled with the Common Core implementation, resulting in a dismal performance on national assessments.

Influence of Teachers' Unions

Teachers' unions wield considerable influence over education policy, often to the detriment of students. They lobby against merit-based pay and resist efforts to hold teachers accountable for student performance. In many cases, unions protect underperforming teachers from being fired, leading to a stagnation in educational quality. A study by the National Bureau of Economic Research found that stronger teachers' unions correlate with lower student achievement, particularly in liberal states where these unions are most powerful
.

Specific Legislative Examples

Specific legislative examples illustrate the impact of these policies. The Every Student Succeeds Act (ESSA) aimed to provide more flexibility to states, but critics argue it hasn't done enough to improve educational outcomes. Similarly, California's Proposition 30, which increased taxes to fund education, has seen mixed results, with little improvement in student performance despite the influx of cash.

The Data Doesn't Lie

According to NCES data, public schools in cities like Chicago, Detroit, and Washington D.C. consistently underperform compared to national averages. For instance, in 2022, only 21% of Detroit's 8th graders were proficient in math, and just 14% were proficient in reading. In Chicago, less than a quarter of 11th graders met college readiness benchmarks in reading and math.

Wrapping Up the Sinking Ship

So, what's the takeaway? Liberal policies, despite their noble intentions, often exacerbate the problems they aim to solve in public education. From teacher unions to funding disparities and curriculum changes, these policies have turned our education system into a sinking ship. And until we address the root causes and implement effective reforms, we'll keep bailing water without ever staying afloat.

Undeniable Facts

1. **Historical milestones in public education:**
    ◦ **1647:** The Massachusetts Bay Colony passed the Old

Deluder Satan Act, requiring towns to establish schools.
- **1954:** The Supreme Court's landmark decision in Brown v. Board of Education declared state laws establishing separate public schools for black and white students to be unconstitutional.
- **1975:** The Education for All Handicapped Children Act (now IDEA) was enacted, ensuring services to children with disabilities throughout the nation.

2. **Notable education reforms and their outcomes:**
- **No Child Left Behind Act (2001):** Aimed to close achievement gaps, but faced criticism for its emphasis on standardized testing, leading to its replacement by the Every Student Succeeds Act (ESSA) in 2015.
- **Common Core State Standards (2010):** Intended to standardize educational outcomes, but faced backlash for implementation issues and perceived rigidity.

3. **Quotes about the state of public education:**
- "Education is the most powerful weapon which you can use to change the world." - Nelson Mandela.
- "The roots of education are bitter, but the fruit is sweet." - Aristotle.
- "Education is what remains after one has forgotten what one has learned in school." - Albert Einstein.

4. **Surprising facts about education funding:**
- The U.S. spends more per student than most other countries, yet often lags in educational performance metrics.
- Despite receiving federal funds, many urban school districts face severe budget shortfalls, leading to resource disparities and underfunded classrooms.

5. **Fun facts about school systems around the world:**
- In Finland, students start school at age 7 and have shorter school days and fewer homework assignments, yet consistently rank high in global education assessments.
- In Japan, students participate in daily cleaning activities as

part of their curriculum, instilling a sense of responsibility and community.

6. **Key legislative bills related to public education:**
   - **Elementary and Secondary Education Act (ESEA) of 1965:** Provided federal funding to primary and secondary education, emphasizing equal access to education.
   - **Individuals with Disabilities Education Act (IDEA) of 1990:** Ensured students with disabilities are provided with Free Appropriate Public Education that is tailored to their individual needs.

7. **Dates and outcomes of major education initiatives:**
   - **Race to the Top (2009):** Offered competitive grants to encourage and reward states for education innovation and reform, but its effectiveness remains debated.
   - **Every Student Succeeds Act (ESSA) of 2015:** Replaced No Child Left Behind, giving more flexibility to states in their educational standards and accountability systems.

8. **Notable politicians involved in education policies:**
   - **Horace Mann:** Known as the "Father of American Public Education," he advocated for universal, non-sectarian, and free schooling.
   - **Arne Duncan:** Served as U.S. Secretary of Education under President Obama, promoting policies like Race to the Top and Common Core.

9. **Comparisons of education performance between liberal and conservative states:**
   - Liberal states like Massachusetts and New Jersey often rank high in national education performance metrics, partially due to higher funding and rigorous standards.
   - Conservative states like Texas and Florida also show strong performance, focusing on standardized testing and accountability measures.

10. **Case studies of specific education policies and their impacts:**
    - **New York City's Renewal Schools Program:** Aimed to

turn around struggling schools with additional resources and support, but was ultimately deemed a failure due to lack of significant improvement in student outcomes.

- **Chicago's charter school expansion:** Seen as a mixed success, with some charter schools outperforming public counterparts, while others show no significant difference in performance.

5 - Crime and Punishment in Blue Cities

Step inside the twisted carnival of modern urban life, where crime rates rise and fall like a particularly infuriating game of Whac-A-Mole. Just when you think you've got one crime spree under control, another pops up to take its place. Where does this chaos thrive the most? In the heart of America's blue cities, thanks to liberal policies that seem to be as effective at controlling crime as a paper umbrella in a hurricane.

Analyzing the Increase in Crime Rates in Liberal Cities

First, let's look at the numbers. Over the past few years, cities like Chicago, Baltimore, and San Francisco have seen a disturbing uptick in crime rates that can only be described as alarming.

Chicago, known for its deep-dish pizza and deep-set crime problems, saw its murder rate increase by 55% from 2019 to 2020. This surge wasn't confined to just one area but was spread across the city, affecting neighborhoods from Englewood to Lincoln Park. The city also experienced a 50% increase in shootings, with over 4,000 incidents reported in 2020, compared to 2,700 in 2019. The rise in violent crime has stretched the city's police force thin, leading to longer response times and an atmosphere of growing insecurity among residents.

Baltimore, another poster child for urban chaos, has been grappling with some of the highest per capita murder rates in the country. In 2020, Baltimore reported 335 homicides, marking the sixth consecutive year with over 300 murders. The city's struggles with drug-related violence and gang activities have only compounded the issue. Despite various crime reduction initiatives, including community policing and increased funding for violence interruption programs, the city has seen little improvement. The per capita murder rate here is staggeringly high, making Baltimore one of the most dangerous cities in America.

San Francisco, despite its picturesque views and tech-driven prosperity, reported a 17% increase in property crimes in 2021. This includes a sharp rise in car break-ins, burglaries, and retail thefts. Neighborhoods like the Tenderloin and SoMa have become notorious for their high crime rates. Even affluent areas such as Nob Hill and Pacific Heights haven't been immune to the crime wave.

The city's lenient approach to petty crimes, influenced by progressive policies, has led to a situation where residents and business owners feel increasingly vulnerable. Retailers, in particular, have voiced concerns over organized theft rings that operate with impunity, exploiting the gaps in enforcement created by policy changes.

By examining these cities, we can see an obvious pattern: progressive policies, though well-intentioned, appear to correlate with a rise in crime rates. This isn't just about statistics; it's about the lived experiences of millions of residents who now face daily uncertainties about their safety. The policies intended to reform and rehabilitate are often criticized for inadvertently creating environments where crime can flourish. The data from these cities provides a stark illustration of how theory and practice can diverge, leading to real-world consequences that affect everyday life.

The Role of Liberal Policies

What's fueling this rise? Let's uncover the political truth.

1. **Defunding the Police**: This well-intentioned but arguably misguided policy has led to reduced police budgets and fewer officers on the streets. The result? A vacuum of law enforcement that criminals are all too happy to fill. Fewer officers mean slower response times and less deterrence.

2. **Bail Reform**: Take New York's bail reform laws, for instance. Designed to eliminate cash bail for most misdemeanors and non-violent felonies, these reforms have inadvertently allowed repeat offenders to return to the streets almost immediately. It's like giving a free pass to the Whac-A-Mole malcontents to pop back up as soon as you smack them down.

3. **Lenient Sentencing**: California's Proposition 47, which reclassified certain felonies as misdemeanors, has been criticized for contributing to rising crime rates. By reducing the penalties for various crimes, the proposition effectively lowered the stakes for criminal behavior. Consequently, crimes with severe penalties are now lightly punished.

Real-World Examples and Data

HOW TO UNDERSTAND LEFT-WING POLITICAL SPIN

To bring the point home, let's dive into some specific examples and data. The FBI's Uniform Crime Reporting (UCR) program provides a treasure trove of statistics that reveal the stark reality of rising crime rates in liberal cities.

In **San Francisco**, according to the UCR, violent crime increased by 5.4% from 2019 to 2020. This rise includes a significant uptick in assaults and robberies, reflecting the growing sense of lawlessness in certain areas. Reports of aggravated assaults jumped by nearly 10%, highlighting the increasing danger faced by residents and visitors alike. The property crime rate, encompassing theft and burglary, has also seen a sharp increase, with vehicle break-ins becoming almost a rite of passage for anyone daring to park on city streets.

Chicago's situation is even more dire. The city's police department reported over 770 homicides in 2020, a stark increase from the previous year, when the number was around 500. This surge represents a 55% rise in homicides, making it one of the deadliest years in recent history. Shootings in Chicago also soared, with over 4,000 incidents reported. This alarming trend has overwhelmed local law enforcement and emergency services, leading to prolonged response times and decreased community trust in public safety institutions. The ripple effect on the city's social fabric is profound, with families and neighborhoods grappling with the trauma of persistent violence.

Baltimore continues to struggle despite many initiatives aimed at curbing violence. According to local police data, there were 335 homicides in 2020, marking the sixth consecutive year with over 300 murders. This stubbornly high murder rate underscores the challenges faced by the city in addressing deep-rooted issues such as poverty, drug addiction, and gang violence. Efforts like community policing and violence interruption programs, while noble, have so far failed to produce significant declines in crime. The city's per capita murder rate remains one of the highest in the nation, painting a grim picture of the effectiveness of current policies and initiatives.

These numbers paint a stark and sobering picture of the effectiveness of the liberal policies currently in place. Despite the good intentions behind reforms like defunding the police, bail reform, and lenient sentencing, the data suggests these measures may contribute to an environment where crime can flourish unchecked. New York's bail reform law, enacted in 2020, aimed to eliminate cash bail for most misdemeanors and non-violent felonies, but has faced criticism for enabling repeat offenders and increasing repeat offenses.

California's Proposition 47, passed in 2014, downgraded several non-violent crimes, including drug possession and theft of property under $950, from felonies to misdemeanors. While intended to reduce prison populations and address systemic inequities, it has inadvertently led to a decrease in arrests and prosecutions for these offenses. As a result, many argue that it has emboldened criminals and led to an increase in crime rates, particularly in urban areas.

In summary, while these policies might be rooted in noble intentions, their real-world impacts suggest they may be more akin to playing Whac-A-Mole with our safety. Each legislative "reform" seems to pop up with new, unintended consequences, leaving citizens to navigate a landscape where the only certainty is uncertainty.

Legislative Examples

New York's bail reform law, enacted in 2020, eliminated cash-bail for most misdemeanors and non-violent felonies. While intended to address inequities in the justice system, it has faced criticism for allowing offenders to return to the streets too quickly, contributing to a rise in repeat offenses.

California's Proposition 47, passed in 2014, downgraded several non-violent crimes, including drug possession and theft of property under $950, from felonies to misdemeanors. This has led to fewer arrests and prosecutions for these offenses, which many argue has emboldened criminals and led to an increase in crime.

In summary, while these policies might be rooted in noble intentions, their real-world impacts suggest they may be more akin to playing Whac-A-Mole with our safety. Each legislative "reform" seems to pop up with new, unintended consequences, leaving citizens to navigate a landscape where the only certainty is uncertainty.

Undeniable Facts:

1. Historical Crime Trends in Major Cities

Crime trends have fluctuated over the decades, influenced by various social, economic, and political factors. For example, the 1990s saw a significant drop in crime rates across many major U.S. cities, often attributed to enhanced policing strategies and economic growth. However, recent years have seen a troubling reversal of this trend, particularly in cities with progressive policies.

2. Notable Crime Waves and Their Causes

Chicago's infamous crime wave in the 1920s, driven by Prohibition and organized crime, led to the rise of notorious figures like Al Capone. More recently, the opioid crisis has fueled a new wave of drug-related crimes in many urban areas, highlighting the ongoing battle between law enforcement and evolving criminal enterprises.

3. Famous Quotes About Crime and Punishment

Cicero once said, "The more laws, the less justice." This ancient wisdom resonates today, reminding us that well-intentioned legislation can sometimes complicate the pursuit of justice. Another pertinent quote from Albert Einstein is, "The world is a dangerous place, not because of those who do evil, but because of those who look on and do nothing."

4. Surprising Crime Statistics from Various Cities

In 2020, Los Angeles reported a 30% increase in homicides compared to the previous year, despite its reputation as a progressive city with many social programs. Meanwhile, Portland saw a staggering 800% rise in homicides in the same period, reflecting the city's struggles with public safety amidst widespread protests and calls for police reform.

5. Fun Facts About Law Enforcement Practices

Did you know that the first organized police force in the United States was established in Boston in 1838? Or that New York City's police department, the largest in the country, employs over 36,000 officers? These tidbits highlight the long history and scale of law enforcement efforts in America.

6. Key Legislative Bills Related to Crime and Policing

Notable reforms include New York's Bail Reform Law, which aimed to address systemic issues but has faced criticism and challenges in implementation. Another important legislative effort, the Fair Sentencing Act of 2010, focused on reducing racial disparities in drug sentencing. California's Proposition 47, while intended to reduce the state's prison population and redirect funds to rehabilitation programs, inadvertently led to a spike in petty crimes, highlighting the complexity of implementing such reforms. Similarly, the Sentencing Reform and Corrections Act of 2015 proposed reducing mandatory minimum sentences for certain non-violent drug offenses and encouraged the use of alternative sentencing methods like drug courts.

7. Dates and Outcomes of Major Crime Prevention Initiatives

The "Broken Windows" policing strategy, implemented in New York City in the 1990s, focused on cracking down on minor offenses to prevent more serious crimes. This initiative is credited with contributing to a significant drop in crime during that decade. However, its legacy is debated, with critics arguing it led to over-policing and strained community relations.

8. Notable Politicians Known for Their Crime Policies

Rudy Giuliani, former Mayor of New York City, is often credited with reducing crime through aggressive policing strategies. Conversely, Kim Foxx, the State's Attorney for Cook County, Illinois, has faced criticism for her progressive policies, which some argue have contributed to rising crime rates in Chicago.

9. Comparisons of Crime Rates Between Liberal and Conservative Cities

A 2021 analysis showed that liberal cities like San Francisco and Seattle had higher rates of property crimes compared to conservative cities like Mesa, Arizona, and Plano, Texas. This comparison suggests that differing political philosophies on crime and punishment can lead to varied outcomes in public safety.

10. Case Studies of Specific Crime Policies and Their Impacts

Case studies, such as implementing "stop-and-frisk" in New York City, reveal the complex effects of specific crime policies. While this policy led to a decrease in crime rates, it also sparked significant controversy over racial profiling and civil liberties. Another example is Seattle's approach to decriminalizing drug possession, which aimed to reduce incarceration rates but has faced criticism for failing to address the root causes of addiction and associated crimes.

Bottom line, these undeniable facts illustrate the multifaceted nature of crime and punishment in America's blue cities. Understanding these elements is crucial for anyone looking to navigate the complexities of modern urban safety and criminal justice.

The Failures of Progressive Criminal Justice Reform

Progressive criminal justice reforms are often implemented with noble intentions: to create a fairer, more equitable system. However, these reforms frequently lead to unintended negative consequences, much like trying to fix a leaky faucet with duct tape—it may seem like a good idea at first, but soon you're dealing with a flooded kitchen.

Unintended Consequences of Progressive Criminal Justice Reforms

One of the most prominent examples of these unintended consequences is **bail reform**. The idea behind bail reform is to eliminate the inequity of the cash bail system, which disproportionately affects low-income individuals. New York City's bail reform law, enacted in 2020, aimed to ensure that people aren't jailed simply because they can't afford bail. However, this well-meaning reform has had some serious repercussions. According to the Bureau of Justice Statistics (BJS), there has been a notable increase in repeat offenses among individuals released under the new bail system. Data shows that re-arrests for crimes such as burglary and assault have risen by over 20% since the reform's implementation.

In California, **Proposition 47**, passed in 2014, reclassified several non-violent offenses, such as drug possession and theft of property under $950, from felonies to misdemeanors. The proposition was designed to reduce the state's prison population and redirect funds to rehabilitation programs. However, an academic study from the University of California found that while the prison population did decrease, there was a significant uptick in petty crimes, particularly theft and drug-related offenses. This rise in crime has been felt acutely by small business owners and residents, who now face higher rates of shoplifting and vandalism.

Another significant reform effort involves **police funding cuts**. The movement to defund the police gained momentum in several cities, aiming to reallocate funds to community services and social programs. While the intention is to address the root causes of crime, such as poverty and lack of mental health services, the immediate consequence has often been a rise in crime rates. For instance, Minneapolis, which significantly cut its police budget in 2020, experienced a 30% increase in violent crimes the following year. This includes a sharp rise in homicides, carjackings, and assaults.

To further illustrate these points, let's delve into some specific examples:

1. **New York City's Bail Reform**: Since the reform's enactment, there have been many instances where individuals released without bail committed additional crimes while awaiting trial. For example, one study found that re-arrest rates for burglary and assault among

released individuals increased by 20% in the year following the reform. This has raised concerns about public safety and the adequacy of the reform's implementation.

2. **California's Proposition 47**: The decriminalization of certain offenses has led to a noticeable increase in petty crimes. According to the Bureau of Justice Statistics, thefts and drug offenses spiked by 25% in some California cities after the passage of Proposition 47. Small businesses have particularly felt the brunt, with a significant rise in shoplifting incidents reported.

3. **Police Funding Cuts in Minneapolis**: The city's decision to cut its police budget resulted in a noticeable increase in crime. Homicides rose by 30%, and carjackings saw a staggering 537% increase in the year following the cuts. These statistics highlight the unintended consequences of reducing police presence without adequate alternative measures in place.

Imagine progressive criminal justice reform efforts as trying to fix a leaky faucet with duct tape. At first, it seems like a clever, cost-effective solution. However, the tape eventually fails, leaving behind a mess that is even worse. The water's everywhere, and now you not only have to fix the original leak but also clean up the unintended flood it caused. Similarly, while the intention behind these reforms is commendable, the execution often leads to a cascade of unforeseen problems, leaving communities to deal with the aftermath.

To connect all the dots on this issue, while progressive criminal justice reforms aim to address systemic inequities, the reality is that they often result in unintended negative consequences. By examining the data and specific examples, it becomes clear that these reforms need careful consideration and balanced implementation to truly achieve their intended goals without compromising public safety.

Undeniable Facts

The **Sentencing Reform Act of 1984** aimed to reduce disparities in sentencing by introducing mandatory minimum sentences. While it sought to create a fairer system, it led to a significant increase in the prison population and sparked ongoing debates about fairness and effectiveness.

Notable Failures and Successes in Criminal Justice Reform

The Fair Sentencing Act of 2010 successfully addressed racial disparities by reducing the crack and powder cocaine sentence disparity.

On the other hand, **California's Proposition 47** is often cited as a failure. Passed in 2014, it reclassified certain non-violent crimes as misdemeanors, which reduced the prison population but led to an increase in petty crimes like shoplifting.

Quotes About the Challenges of Criminal Justice Reform

"Justice delayed is justice denied." – William E. Gladstone

"The arc of the moral universe is long, but it bends towards justice." – Martin Luther King Jr.

Interesting Facts About Prison and Parole Systems

The United States has the highest incarceration rate in the world, with over 2.1 million people currently in prison or jail. This high number results from policies such as mandatory minimum sentences, three-strikes laws, and a general emphasis on punitive measures over rehabilitation. The U.S. system prioritizes long sentences and incarceration as primary methods of deterring crime and punishing offenders.

In contrast, Norway takes a fundamentally different approach to criminal justice. The maximum prison sentence in Norway is 21 years, with the possibility of extension if the individual is still considered a threat to society. Norway focuses heavily on rehabilitation, aiming to reintegrate offenders into society as productive citizens.

Prisons are designed to be humane, emphasizing education, vocational training, and therapeutic support. This approach reflects a belief that treating offenders with dignity and providing them with skills and support can reduce recidivism and benefit society as a whole.

While the U.S. system results in high incarceration rates and ongoing debates about fairness and effectiveness, Norway's system leads to lower recidivism rates and a more humane approach to justice.

Fun Facts About Criminal Justice Practices Around the World

In Japan, the conviction rate is over 99%, largely because of the extensive use of confessions, often obtained under prolonged detention. Meanwhile, the Netherlands has closed many of its prisons in recent years due to a significant decrease in crime rates and an emphasis on rehabilitation.

Key Legislative Bills Related to Criminal Justice Reform

The **First Step Act of 2018** aimed to reform the federal prison system and reduce recidivism. It included provisions for early release and rehabilitation programs and expanded judges' discretion in sentencing for certain offenses.

Another important legislative effort, the **Fair Sentencing Act of 2010**, focused on reducing racial disparities in drug sentencing.

California's Proposition 47, while intended to reduce the state's prison population and redirect funds to rehabilitation programs, inadvertently led to a spike in petty crimes, highlighting the complexity of implementing such reforms.

Similarly, the **Sentencing Reform and Corrections Act of 2015** proposed reducing mandatory minimum sentences for certain non-violent drug offenses and encouraged the use of alternative sentencing methods like drug courts.

The **Juvenile Justice Reform Act of 2018** reauthorized and updated the Juvenile Justice and Delinquency Prevention Act of 1974. It focused on improving conditions of confinement for juvenile offenders and promoting evidence-based practices and alternatives to incarceration.

Meanwhile, **New York's Bail Reform Law of 2020** aimed to eliminate cash bail for most misdemeanors and non-violent felonies, but it faced criticism for allowing repeat offenders to return to the streets quickly.

The **Violent Crime Control and Law Enforcement Act of 1994** introduced tougher sentencing. It included the "three strikes" mandatory life sentence for repeat offenders, and increased funding for law enforcement, resulting in a significant increase in the prison population.

In 1994, the **Violent Crime Control and Law Enforcement Act** introduced tougher sentencing and increased law enforcement funding, leading to a rise in the prison population. Similarly, **California's Proposition 47** in 2014 aimed to reduce the prison population by reclassifying non-violent felonies as misdemeanors, though it raised concerns about increased petty crime.

Kamala Harris, as California's Attorney General, introduced several reforms aimed at reducing recidivism and promoting rehabilitation. **Rand Paul** has been an advocate for reducing mandatory minimum sentences and addressing disparities in the criminal justice system.

Liberal states like California and New York have focused on decriminalization and rehabilitation, leading to reduced prison populations but facing criticism for rising crime rates. Conservative states like Texas have implemented tough-on-crime policies, resulting in higher incarceration rates but also lower crime rates in some areas.

New York Bail Reform, enacted in 2020, aimed to eliminate cash bail for most misdemeanors and non-violent felonies. While it reduced the pretrial detention population, it faced backlash due to a perceived increase in repeat offenses.

Over the past decade, **Texas has implemented various reforms**, such as drug courts and diversion programs. These initiatives have reduced the state's prison population, saved billions of dollars, and continued to see a decline in crime rates.

6 - Unmasking the Myths

In this chapter, we'll unravel the tangled web of political spin and media misrepresentation. Armed with facts and a sharp sense of humor, we'll expose the truth behind 40 of the most infamous political narratives. By the end, you'll be able to spot spin from a mile away and enjoy a good laugh at the absurdity of it all. It's time to debunk some myths, so buckle up!

1. The Clinton Foundation Scandal

Official Narrative:

The Clinton Foundation is a model of charitable work, funneling donations to those in need. The media highlighted their global impact and praised their transparency, showcasing heartwarming stories of lives transformed by their initiatives.

What Really Happened:

Investigations revealed most donations covered administrative costs and lavish events, with questionable foreign donations raising ethical concerns. The foundation was more of a pricey showroom than Santa's workshop. Funds intended for charity often ended up lining the pockets of the Clintons and their associates, making their "charitable" efforts a well-oiled money machine rather than a beacon of altruism.

2. Benghazi Incident

Official Narrative:

The 2012 attack on the U.S. consulate in Benghazi was a spontaneous protest over an anti-Islam video. The White House emphasized the unpredictable nature of the incident, and the media echoed this narrative, portraying it as a sudden eruption of violence with no prior warning.

What Really Happened:

It was a planned terrorist attack, with ignored warnings and poor security measures. Ambassador Chris Stevens, Sean Smith, Glen Doherty, and Tyrone Woods were killed in the attack. Secretary of State Hillary Clinton's involvement in the incident was downplayed, despite emails showing she was well aware of the risks. Even today, she refuses to accept any responsibility and remains unapologetic, a stance that unravels the official story faster than a cheap sweater.

3. IRS Targeting Scandal

Official Narrative:

The IRS's scrutiny of tax-exempt status applications was presented as routine compliance. Media reports suggested it was a standard procedure affecting all groups equally, with no political bias.

What Really Happened:

Conservative groups were disproportionately targeted, delaying their applications and limiting their political activities. The scandal was like borrowing a lawnmower to start a landscaping business without permission. The IRS's actions were politically motivated, aiming to stifle conservative voices during a critical election period.

4. Obamacare Promises

Official Narrative:

"If you like your healthcare plan, you can keep it," assured President Obama. The media echoed this promise to calm public concerns, emphasizing the stability and improvement the Affordable Care Act would bring.

What Really Happened:

Millions lost their existing plans, revealing this promise was as reliable as a chocolate teapot. The rollout of Obamacare was a classic bait-and-switch, with many Americans facing higher premiums and fewer choices. The reality was a far cry from the rosy picture painted by the administration and its media cheerleaders.

5. Economic Stimulus Impact

Official Narrative:

Stimulus packages would significantly boost the economy and reduce unemployment. Government officials promised quick and substantial benefits, with media reports highlighting projected job creation and economic growth.

What Really Happened:

The effects were mixed at best, with benefits often overstated. Expecting a firework display but getting a sparkler, the stimulus packages failed to deliver the promised economic boom. Many funds were mis-allocated, and the long-term impact on the national debt was downplayed, leaving taxpayers to foot the bill.

6. Fast and Furious Operation

Official Narrative:

The gun-walking program aimed to track firearms to Mexican cartels, intending to dismantle criminal networks. It was presented as a strategic law enforcement initiative, with media coverage highlighting its bold approach to curbing gun violence.

What Really Happened:

The operation lost track of weapons, which were used in crimes, including the killing of a U.S. Border Patrol agent. A plan more misguided than a blindfolded dart throw, Fast and Furious exposed the incompetence and recklessness of those in charge. The fallout included congressional investigations and a deep mistrust in federal law enforcement's handling of such operations.

7. Russian Collusion Narrative

Official Narrative:

The Trump campaign colluded with Russia in the 2016 election to influence the outcome. Media reports were filled with speculative accusations and ominous implications, suggesting a vast conspiracy orchestrated by the Kremlin.

What Really Happened:

Multiple investigations, including the Mueller Report, found insufficient evidence of collusion. The narrative was more of a political witch hunt than a spy thriller, with endless media speculation creating more smoke than fire. The frenzy distracted from real issues, showcasing the media's propensity for sensationalism over substance.

8. Immigration Policy Misrepresentations

Official Narrative:

Policies intended to keep borders secure were labeled draconian by critics. The media often portrayed them as unprecedented and excessively harsh, focusing on emotional stories of separated families and humanitarian crises. Reports highlighted heart-wrenching images and stories of desperate migrants, painting a picture of unnecessary cruelty and inhumanity at the border.

What Really Happened:

The reality of U.S. border policy is far more complex and dire than the mainstream narrative suggests. Over the years, millions of illegal immigrants, including known criminals and potential terrorists, have crossed into the country. The Obama administration deported record numbers of immigrants, yet media criticism was relatively muted compared to later administrations.

When Trump took office, his more stringent immigration policies were met with fierce backlash, and his "zero tolerance" policy, which led to family separations, became a focal point of media outrage. Yet, many of these policies were extensions or enhancements of existing laws that had been inadequately enforced for years.

Under Biden, the border crisis has reached unprecedented levels. Despite claims that the "border is closed," daily footage shows tens of thousands pouring over the border. This massive influx includes not just families seeking a better life but also dangerous criminals and potential terrorists exploiting the chaos. The Biden administration's policies, or lack thereof, have effectively created an open-border situation, leading to overwhelmed border facilities and communities.

The sheer scale of illegal immigration under the Biden administration has been staggering, with estimates of over two million illegal crossings in 2021 alone. Critics argue that this appears intentional, given the preventability of the situation if existing laws were enforced. Not only do the humanitarian implications of the administration's failure to control the border raise concerns, but there are also national security risks at stake.

The media's portrayal often glosses over these facts, focusing instead on the narrative of the humanitarian crisis without addressing the systemic failures and deliberate policy choices contributing to the problem. The ongoing border situation highlights a broken immigration system that successive administrations have failed to fix, exacerbated by policies that seem more about political posturing than effective governance.

This issue isn't just a policy failure; it's a national crisis with long-term implications for security, economy, and social cohesion. The insistence by some on the left that the "border is closed" in the face of overwhelming evidence to the contrary is an obvious example of political spin at its finest. The disconnect between official narratives and on-the-ground realities has left many Americans disillusioned and frustrated with their leaders' inability to safeguard the nation's borders.

9. Wikileaks Revelations
Official Narrative:

Under the Obama administration, Wikileaks documents were dismissed as misleading or false by officials. The media downplayed their significance, suggesting they were manipulated or obtained through nefarious means. Reports focused on the dubious nature of the leaks rather than the content, portraying Julian Assange and his organization as threats to national security.

What Really Happened:

The documents revealed uncomfortable truths and hidden agendas, exposing political corruption, media bias, and unethical practices within the government. Emails from the Democratic National Committee (DNC) showed favoritism towards Hillary Clinton over Bernie Sanders during the 2016 primaries. These revelations shattered the facade of impartiality, leading to resignations within the DNC and public outrage. The leaks also uncovered questionable foreign policy decisions and surveillance practices, showing a government more interested in controlling narratives than addressing misconduct. Like finding out your favorite restaurant has a rodent problem, the Wikileaks revelations forced the public to confront the unsavory reality behind polished political rhetoric.

10. COVID-19 Policy Decisions

Official Narrative:

Early pandemic policies were based on the best science and aimed at public safety. Officials emphasized their swift and decisive action, with the media supporting these efforts as necessary and prudent. From social distancing to mask mandates, every measure was portrayed as a critical step in controlling the virus's spread.

What Really Happened:

The reality was far different and far more chaotic. Many early decisions were based on incomplete or faulty science, leading to widespread misinformation. For instance, the six-foot social distancing rule was pulled out of thin air—no substantial evidence supported it. It was a measure designed more for public reassurance than effectiveness.

Mask mandates were another contentious issue. Initially, masks were deemed unnecessary by health officials, including Dr. Anthony Fauci. Later, they became essential, despite emerging studies showing that masks, particularly cloth ones, were largely ineffective at preventing COVID-19 transmission. The mixed messages led to public confusion and mistrust, with many feeling like they were being taken for a ride on a rollercoaster of contradictory guidelines.

The infamous "two weeks to flatten the curve" turned into months of lockdowns, devastating the economy and small businesses while providing no clear end in sight. These lockdowns were based on models and projections that vastly overestimated the virus's lethality and spread. Countries and states with varying degrees of lockdown measures did not show consistent outcomes, further questioning the necessity and efficacy of such draconian measures.

Vaccination policies also sparked controversy. While vaccines were hailed as the ultimate solution, their rollout was marred by inconsistent messaging and political infighting. The push for vaccine mandates ignored natural immunity and prior infection, leading to resistance and division within the population. Booster shots were added to the confusion, as their necessity and frequency kept changing.

Moreover, the treatment of dissenting voices and alternative viewpoints was alarming. Scientists and doctors who questioned the mainstream narrative were often censored or discredited, stifling open debate and scientific inquiry. The media played a significant role in perpetuating fear, sensationalizing the pandemic, and suppressing counter-narratives.

The pandemic response also exposed the limits of government competence. Bureaucratic inefficiencies led to shortages of essential supplies, such as personal protective equipment (PPE) and ventilators. The rollout of testing and contact tracing was inconsistent and often ineffective. Public health agencies, overwhelmed and under-prepared, struggled to provide clear and consistent guidance.

The handling of the pandemic showcased a staggering level of mismanagement and highlighted deep-seated issues within our public health infrastructure. It was like trying to solve a puzzle with missing pieces, with conflicting messages and uncoordinated efforts leading to widespread frustration and anger. The pandemic didn't just expose the cracks in the system; it revealed gaping chasms of incompetence and political maneuvering that left the public feeling abandoned and misled. While this book is more critical of the left, it must be acknowledged that both parties share many of the shortcomings that were highlighted during the COVID-19 catastrophe.

11. Healthcare.gov Launch
Official Narrative:

Under the Obama administration, the Healthcare.gov website would streamline the enrollment process for millions. The launch was touted as a technological marvel that would simplify access to healthcare, and the media covered it as a monumental step forward. It was hailed as a critical component of the Affordable Care Act, promising easy access and improved healthcare coverage for all Americans.

What Really Happened:

The site crashed repeatedly, plagued by technical issues and poor design. Users encountered error messages and slow load times, making it a nightmare to navigate. Like expecting a luxury car and getting a lemon, the rollout was a disaster that highlighted the government's technological ineptitude. The initial chaos and frustration overshadowed the intended benefits, revealing a rushed and poorly executed project that left many questioning the efficiency of government-led initiatives.

12. Solyndra Scandal

Official Narrative:

Under the Obama administration, Solyndra was a shining example of green energy innovation, heavily endorsed by the administration. The investment was expected to lead to job creation and energy breakthroughs, and the media painted it as a win for the future of sustainable energy. The company was showcased as a model for how government investment could drive the green economy forward.

What Really Happened:

The company went bankrupt, wasting over half a billion dollars in taxpayer money. It was a solar-powered flop, with mismanagement and unrealistic projections leading to its downfall. The scandal exposed the pitfalls of government-backed ventures into the private sector, where political motives often overshadow practical realities. Instead of a green energy revolution, Solyndra became a cautionary tale of how poor oversight and political grandstanding can lead to spectacular financial failures.

13. VA Hospital Scandal

Official Narrative:

Under both the Bush and Obama administrations, VA hospitals were portrayed as providing top-notch care to veterans. Officials highlighted their commitment to serving those who served, and the media praised the VA's efforts to improve healthcare for veterans. The narrative emphasized increased funding and expanded services as indicators of the system's success.

What Really Happened:

Reports of long wait times and poor conditions surfaced, revealing systemic neglect. Veterans faced delays in receiving care, sometimes with fatal consequences. More a house of horrors than a haven of care, the scandal showed a gross failure to meet the needs of those who had sacrificed for their country. Whistleblowers and investigations uncovered falsified records and cover-ups, exposing a deeply flawed system that was more concerned with appearances than the well-being of veterans. The scandal highlighted the urgent need for comprehensive reform within the VA healthcare system.

14. Net Neutrality Debate

Official Narrative:

During the Trump administration, the repeal of net neutrality was promoted as a move that would lead to a better, more competitive internet. Proponents claimed it would spur innovation and investment, and the media echoed these optimistic projections. The Federal Communications Commission (FCC) argued that removing the regulations would encourage ISPs to improve infrastructure and services.

What Really Happened:

Critics warned it would allow ISPs to throttle speeds and create paid fast lanes, reducing internet equality. More toll roads than the information superhighway, the repeal raised concerns about access and fairness in the digital age. Small businesses and consumers feared that without net neutrality, large corporations would dominate the internet, stifling competition and innovation. The debate highlighted deep divisions over how best to regulate the internet, with many arguing that the move favored corporate interests over public good.

15. Flint Water Crisis

Official Narrative:

Under the Snyder administration in Michigan, initial reports downplayed the severity of Flint's water contamination, suggesting it was under control. Officials assured residents the water was safe, and the media initially supported these claims, echoing the government's reassurances that the situation was being effectively managed.

What Really Happened:

The water was dangerously contaminated with lead, causing widespread health issues, including developmental problems in children. A toxic truth hidden behind a curtain of lies, the crisis was a stark example of environmental injustice and governmental failure. Residents of Flint suffered from rashes, hair loss, and serious health issues, while officials' assurances turned out to be hollow. Emails and documents later revealed that officials were aware of the contamination long before taking action, prioritizing cost savings over public health. The crisis highlighted systemic issues of neglect and corruption, with vulnerable communities bearing the brunt of the consequences.

16. Syrian Red Line

Official Narrative:

Under the Obama administration, the "red line" on chemical weapons use in Syria was a firm stance against atrocity. The administration promised decisive action if crossed, and the media presented it as a strong deterrent against the Assad regime's use of chemical weapons. This policy was portrayed as a moral and strategic commitment to preventing mass atrocities.

What Really Happened:

When the line was crossed in 2013, with Assad's forces using sarin gas on civilians, the response was tepid and ineffective. A bluff called by a brutal regime, the lack of decisive action undermined U.S. credibility and emboldened adversaries. The red line became a symbol of empty threats in foreign policy, with Assad continuing his brutal campaign largely unchecked. The failure to follow through on promised action revealed the limitations and hesitations of U.S. foreign policy, raising questions about the effectiveness of such public declarations.

17. TARP Fund Effectiveness

Official Narrative:

The Troubled Asset Relief Program (TARP) would stabilize the economy and protect jobs. Officials hailed it as a necessary and effective intervention, with the media highlighting its role in averting economic disaster.

What Really Happened:

While it prevented total collapse, the program was criticized for benefiting big banks over average citizens. More a band-aid on a broken leg, TARP did little to address the underlying issues that led to the financial crisis. The relief was unevenly distributed, sparking debates about fairness and accountability.

18. NSA Surveillance

Official Narrative:

Under the Bush and Obama administrations, NSA surveillance was portrayed as limited and targeted, essential for national security. Assurances were made that privacy was protected, and the media often portrayed it as a necessary evil to prevent terrorist attacks and protect the homeland.

What Really Happened:

Revelations by Edward Snowden in 2013 showed widespread, indiscriminate surveillance, far beyond what the public had been told. Big Brother was watching more than we knew, with the NSA collecting vast amounts of data on ordinary citizens, including phone calls, emails, and internet activity. The disclosures ignited a fierce debate about privacy, security, and government overreach, revealing the extent of government intrusion into private lives and sparking global outrage. The scandal exposed the significant gap between the official narrative and the reality of a surveillance state, raising critical questions about civil liberties in the digital age.

19. Green Jobs Initiative

Official Narrative:

Under the Obama administration, the green jobs initiative was promoted as a strategy that would create millions of sustainable jobs and boost the economy. The administration touted it as a win-win for employment and the environment, and the media supported these optimistic forecasts, celebrating the potential for a new era of green economic growth.

What Really Happened:

Many projects failed, and job creation fell significantly short of promises. More green washed than green revolution, the initiative highlighted the challenges of transitioning to a green economy. Overly ambitious projections and poor implementation led to disillusionment as funds were wasted on unviable projects. The gap between rhetoric and reality left many questioning the effectiveness of government intervention in driving sustainable job growth, revealing the complexities and obstacles in achieving green economic transformation.

20. North Korea Negotiations

Official Narrative:

During both the Obama and Trump administrations, negotiations with North Korea were portrayed as progressing towards denuclearization. Officials claimed significant diplomatic achievements, and the media portrayed these talks as breakthroughs in peace efforts, suggesting a new era of stability on the Korean Peninsula.

What Really Happened:

North Korea continued its nuclear development, and agreements fell apart. Diplomacy proved as effective as a paper umbrella in a monsoon, exposing the difficulty of dealing with a rogue state. Despite high-profile summits and optimistic statements, North Korea's commitment to denuclearization was, at best, superficial. The reality check showed that promises of peace were often more hopeful than practical, as the regime continued to advance its nuclear capabilities while extracting concessions without making genuine concessions of its own. The saga highlighted the complexities and limitations of diplomatic engagement with a regime known for its duplicity and unpredictability.

21. George Soros and Liberal Agendas

Official Narrative:

George Soros is a philanthropist dedicated to promoting democracy, human rights, and liberal causes worldwide. The media often portrays him as a benevolent figure whose contributions foster positive social change.

What Really Happened:

Soros has funded numerous progressive initiatives and political campaigns, often shaping policy outcomes in various countries. Critics argue his influence is more about pushing a specific political agenda than altruism, raising concerns about the extent of his control over democratic processes. The strategic placement of funds to influence elections and policies suggests a calculated effort to mold political landscapes to fit his vision.

22. Obama's Birthplace Controversy

Official Narrative:

Barack Obama's birthplace was questioned by political opponents, but his Hawaiian birth certificate confirmed his U.S. citizenship. The media portrayed the controversy as a baseless conspiracy theory fueled by racism.

What Really Happened:

Despite the official release of his birth certificate, the controversy persisted, driven by public figures like Donald Trump. The "birther" movement highlighted deep-seated divisions and mistrust in political figures. The persistent doubt over Obama's birthplace, despite clear evidence, underscored how misinformation and political agendas can sustain unfounded narratives.

23. Veterans Choice Program

Official Narrative:

The Veterans Choice Program, initiated under the Obama administration and expanded under Trump, was designed to provide veterans with timely access to healthcare by allowing them to seek care outside the VA system. The media lauded it as a significant improvement for veteran healthcare.

What Really Happened:

While well-intentioned, the program faced significant implementation challenges, including bureaucratic red tape and inconsistent application across states. Many veterans found it difficult to access the promised benefits, with long wait times and confusion about eligibility. The program highlighted the complexities of reforming veteran healthcare and the gap between policy intentions and real-world execution.

24. Environmental Protection Policies

Official Narrative:

Environmental protection policies under the Obama administration were hailed as significant steps towards combating climate change. Initiatives like the Clean Power Plan were portrayed as essential for reducing carbon emissions and protecting the planet.

What Really Happened:

While these policies aimed at reducing carbon emissions, they often placed heavy burdens on industries, leading to economic pushback and legal challenges. The implementation faced significant hurdles, and many policies were rolled back under subsequent administrations. The debate highlighted the tension between environmental goals and economic realities, with critics arguing that some measures were more symbolic than effective.

25. Operation Choke Point

Official Narrative:

Operation Choke Point, initiated under the Obama administration, aimed to combat fraud by cutting off access to banking services for high-risk businesses. The media portrayed it as a necessary measure to protect consumers from fraudulent enterprises.

What Really Happened:

The program faced criticism for overreach, targeting legitimate businesses along with fraudulent ones. Industries such as payday lending, firearms sales, and others found themselves unfairly restricted, raising concerns about the government's power to influence banking relationships. Operation Choke Point was eventually discontinued, leaving a legacy of controversy over its methods and impact.

26. Corporate Tax Cuts

Official Narrative:

Under the Trump administration, corporate tax cuts were promoted as a strategy to stimulate economic growth and create jobs. The media presented these cuts as beneficial for the economy, emphasizing the trickle-down effect that would purportedly boost wages and employment.

What Really Happened:

While some businesses did increase investments, many used the tax savings for stock buybacks and executive bonuses rather than expanding operations or raising wages. The anticipated broad economic benefits largely failed to materialize, with critics arguing that the tax cuts primarily enriched shareholders and corporate executives. The disparity between the promised economic boost and the actual outcomes highlighted the limitations of supply-side economics and raised concerns about growing income inequality.

27. Quantitative Easing Policies

Official Narrative: The Federal Reserve's quantitative easing (QE) policies were presented as a necessary measure to stabilize the economy after the 2008 financial crisis. Officials and media narratives emphasized that these policies would support economic recovery by increasing money supply and lowering interest rates.

What Really Happened: While QE helped prevent a deeper recession, it also led to significant asset bubbles and wealth inequality. Critics argued that the policy disproportionately benefited the wealthy, who had greater access to financial markets. As a result, the gap between the rich and the poor widened, and long-term economic imbalances were exacerbated. The consequences of QE highlighted the challenges and unintended effects of unconventional monetary policy.

28. Government Bailouts

Official Narrative:

Government bailouts during the 2008 financial crisis were portrayed as necessary to stabilize the economy and prevent further collapse. The media supported the narrative that these interventions were crucial for saving jobs and maintaining financial stability.

What Really Happened:

While the bailouts did prevent a total collapse, they also disproportionately benefited large financial institutions at the expense of taxpayers and smaller businesses. Critics argue that the bailouts rewarded risky behavior by big banks, contributing to long-term economic inequality. The narrative of necessity overshadowed the ethical and economic implications of bailing out the financial elite while many average Americans continued to suffer.

29. Education Reform

Official Narrative:

Education reforms under the Obama administration, including the Race to the Top initiative, were promoted as transformative measures to improve educational outcomes. The media highlighted the potential for these reforms to close achievement gaps and enhance school performance.

What Really Happened:

The implementation of these reforms faced significant challenges, including resistance from teachers' unions and difficulties in standardizing assessments. The focus on testing and accountability sometimes led to unintended consequences, such as teaching to the test and neglecting broader educational goals. The mixed results revealed the complexity of enacting meaningful educational reform and the limitations of top-down approaches.

30. Climate Change Agreements

Official Narrative:

International climate change agreements, such as the Paris Agreement, were heralded as major achievements in the fight against global warming. The Obama administration and the media emphasized the importance of these agreements in uniting countries to address climate change.

What Really Happened:

While the agreements set ambitious targets, enforcement mechanisms were weak, and many countries struggled to meet their commitments. Critics argued that the agreements were more about political posturing than substantive action, with some nations failing to take meaningful steps to reduce emissions. The withdrawal of the U.S. from the Paris Agreement under the Trump administration further highlighted the challenges of maintaining international consensus on climate action.

31. Judicial Appointments

Official Narrative:

Judicial appointments under both the Obama and Trump administrations were portrayed as necessary to maintain a balanced and fair judiciary. Media narratives often focused on the qualifications and ideological leanings of the appointees, emphasizing the importance of filling vacancies promptly.

What Really Happened:

Both administrations used judicial appointments as tools for advancing their political agendas, leading to a highly polarized judiciary. The focus on ideological purity over qualifications sometimes resulted in controversial appointments and contentious confirmation battles. This politicization of the judiciary has undermined public confidence in the courts' impartiality, turning what should be a nonpartisan process into a political battleground.

32. Puerto Rico Hurricane Response

Official Narrative:

The federal response to Hurricane Maria in Puerto Rico was portrayed as swift and effective. Officials highlighted their efforts and successes, and the media initially supported these claims, suggesting that the situation was being managed well.

What Really Happened:

The response was slow and inadequate, leaving many Puerto Ricans without power, clean water, or essential services for months. Reports later revealed significant logistical failures, insufficient resources, and bureaucratic delays. The disparity between the official narrative and the harsh realities on the ground exposed systemic issues in disaster preparedness and response, particularly for marginalized communities.

33. Keystone XL Pipeline

Official Narrative:

The Keystone XL pipeline was promoted as a project that would create jobs and ensure energy independence. Proponents emphasized its economic benefits and downplayed environmental concerns, with the media often reflecting these optimistic projections.

What Really Happened:

The project faced significant opposition from environmentalists and indigenous groups, highlighting the risks of oil spills and climate change. The economic benefits were also questioned, with many jobs being temporary and the long-term environmental costs potentially outweighing the short-term economic gains. The controversy surrounding the pipeline underscored the tensions between energy development and environmental protection.

34. Foreign Aid Effectiveness

Official Narrative:

Foreign aid programs under various administrations have been touted as essential for promoting global stability, democracy, and development. The media often highlights success stories, suggesting that U.S. aid is a vital tool for fostering positive change abroad.

What Really Happened:

While foreign aid has had successes, it has also faced criticism for inefficiency, corruption, and unintended consequences. Funds have sometimes propped up authoritarian regimes or been siphoned off by corrupt officials, failing to reach those in need. The complexity of international aid highlights the challenges of ensuring that funds are used effectively and ethically, raising questions about the overall impact of such programs.

35. Agricultural Subsidies

Official Narrative:

Agricultural subsidies are portrayed as necessary to support farmers and ensure food security. Media coverage often emphasizes the importance of these subsidies for stabilizing prices and protecting the agricultural sector from economic volatility.

What Really Happened:

In practice, subsidies often disproportionately benefit large agribusinesses over small farmers. This has led to market distortions, overproduction of certain crops, and environmental degradation. Critics argue that the subsidy system favors corporate interests and exacerbates inequalities within the agricultural sector, calling for reforms to create a more equitable and sustainable approach.

36. Government Surveillance of Journalists

Official Narrative:

Government surveillance of journalists is typically justified on the grounds of national security. The narrative often suggests that such measures are necessary to prevent leaks of sensitive information and protect the country from potential threats.

What Really Happened:

Surveillance of journalists has raised serious concerns about press freedom and the protection of sources. Cases like the Obama administration's tracking of reporters' phone records highlighted the potential for abuse and the chilling effect on investigative journalism. These actions have sparked debates about the balance between security and civil liberties, emphasizing the need for greater transparency and accountability in government surveillance practices.

37. Renewable Energy Investments

Official Narrative:

Renewable energy investments under various administrations have been promoted as critical for combating climate change and transitioning to a sustainable future. Media often highlights the potential for job creation and economic growth in the green energy sector, painting a picture of an inevitable and beneficial shift towards sustainable energy sources.

What Really Happened:

While renewable energy investments are essential for reducing carbon emissions, they have also faced significant challenges, including high costs, technological hurdles, and inconsistent policy support. Some projects failed due to poor planning, lack of feasibility, and overly optimistic projections. The gap between ambitious goals and practical implementation underscores the complexities of the energy transition, requiring more strategic and coordinated efforts to achieve long-term sustainability. The reality is that the transition to renewable energy is far more nuanced and difficult than the optimistic narratives suggest.

38. Middle East Peace Initiatives

Official Narrative:

Middle East peace initiatives, particularly under the Trump administration, were touted as groundbreaking steps towards achieving lasting peace in the region. Agreements like the Abraham Accords were presented as major diplomatic successes, with media coverage often reflecting this positive outlook.

What Really Happened:

While the Abraham Accords improved relations between Israel and some Arab nations, they did little to address the core issues of the Israeli-Palestinian conflict. The focus on bilateral agreements with Gulf states overshadowed the ongoing struggles and grievances of Palestinians. The long-standing and deeply entrenched conflicts in the Middle East require more comprehensive and inclusive approaches to achieve genuine and lasting peace. The accords, while positive, were more a strategic alignment against common enemies than a true path to regional harmony.

39. Federal Reserve Independence

Official Narrative:

The Federal Reserve is often portrayed as an independent entity, free from political influence, ensuring stable economic policy and financial oversight. Media narratives typically emphasize the importance of this independence for maintaining market confidence and effective monetary policy.

What Really Happened:

In reality, the Fed's decisions are not entirely insulated from political pressures. Political leaders often exert influence over monetary policy decisions, particularly during times of economic crisis. This dynamic can undermine the Fed's credibility and effectiveness, raising questions about the true extent of its independence and the potential for politically motivated economic decisions. The balancing act between policy objectives and political realities reveals the complexities and potential conflicts inherent in the Fed's role.

40. Student Loan Forgiveness

Official Narrative:

Proposals for student loan forgiveness, particularly under the Biden administration, are presented as essential for alleviating the financial burden on millions of Americans. The media often portrays these initiatives as fair and necessary steps to address the student debt crisis and promote economic equity.

What Really Happened:

While student loan forgiveness could provide relief for many borrowers, it also raises concerns about fairness and long-term economic impact. Critics argue that blanket forgiveness does not address the underlying issues of rising tuition costs and the structure of higher education financing. Additionally, the economic burden of widespread forgiveness could shift to taxpayers, including those who have already paid off their loans or did not attend college. The debate underscores the complexity of addressing student debt in a way that is both equitable and sustainable, highlighting the need for comprehensive reform rather than quick fixes.

41. Media Bias and Fake News

Official Narrative: Mainstream media presents unbiased and factual news.

What Really Happened: The 2016 U.S. presidential election and subsequent years highlighted numerous instances of media bias and misinformation. For example, major networks like CNN and MSNBC were often criticized for their coverage of the Trump administration, accused of focusing heavily on negative stories and downplaying positive news. The term "fake news" became prominent, with both sides of the political spectrum accusing the other of spreading misinformation. Reports on the Covington Catholic High School incident and the Jussie Smollett case were notable examples where initial media narratives were later challenged, revealing a tendency for sensationalism and selective reporting.

42. Defund the Police Movement

Official Narrative: Defunding the police will lead to better community relations and reduced violence.

What Really Happened: The movement gained momentum after the death of George Floyd in 2020, with cities like Minneapolis, Seattle, and Portland taking steps to reduce police funding. However, in many of these areas, crime rates, including violent crimes and homicides, saw significant increases. For instance, Minneapolis experienced a 20% increase in homicides in 2021 compared to the previous year. This trend raised concerns about public safety and the practical implications of reducing police presence. The complexities of police reform were underscored, with critics arguing that defunding efforts were more about political posturing than effective solutions.

43. Green New Deal

Official Narrative: The Green New Deal is essential for combating climate change and creating jobs.

What Really Happened: Proposed by Representative Alexandria Ocasio-Cortez and Senator Ed Markey in 2019, the Green New Deal aimed to address climate change and economic inequality. However, its ambitious goals, such as achieving net-zero greenhouse gas emissions within a decade, were met with skepticism. Economists and industry experts criticized the plan's feasibility, pointing out the enormous financial burden it would place on taxpayers. Estimates suggested costs could reach trillions of dollars. The political backlash highlighted the gap between environmental aspirations and economic realities, with many arguing that more pragmatic approaches were needed.

44. Cancel Culture

Official Narrative: Cancel culture holds people accountable for their actions and promotes social justice.

What Really Happened: The rise of cancel culture in the 2010s saw individuals and public figures being ostracized for controversial statements or actions. High-profile cases like comedian Kevin Hart stepping down from hosting the Oscars in 2018 over past tweets and author J.K. Rowling facing backlash for her comments on gender identity exemplified the phenomenon. Critics argued that cancel culture often resulted in mob justice, where accusations led to severe consequences without due process. This trend sparked debates about free speech and the power of social media, with many feeling that cancel culture stifled open discussion and punished dissenting opinions disproportionately.

45. Gender Identity Policies in Schools

Official Narrative: Inclusive gender identity policies in schools protect and support all students.

What Really Happened: Policies allowing students to choose bathrooms and sports teams based on their gender identity were implemented in various states, including California and New York. These measures were intended to promote inclusivity and prevent discrimination. However, they also led to significant controversy and legal challenges. Parents and educators expressed concerns about privacy and fairness, particularly in sports where biological differences could impact competition. The case of Gavin Grimm, a transgender student who sued his school district in Virginia for bathroom access, went to the Supreme Court, highlighting the national divide on the issue. The complexities of implementing these policies underscored the need for nuanced solutions that balance inclusivity with practical considerations.

46. Election Integrity

Official Narrative: The 2020 election was the most secure in history.

What Really Happened: The 2020 U.S. presidential election saw unprecedented mail-in voting due to the COVID-19 pandemic. Officials, including those from the Department of Homeland Security, assured the public that the election was secure, and media outlets echoed this sentiment.

However, allegations of irregularities surfaced, leading to numerous lawsuits and audits, particularly in swing states like Arizona and Georgia. While courts dismissed many claims due to lack of evidence, the controversy fueled widespread skepticism about election integrity. The contentious environment underscored the need for transparent and secure voting processes, as well as the dangers of undermining public trust in electoral systems.

47. Corporate Influence in Politics

Official Narrative: Corporate donations and lobbying are part of a healthy democratic process.

What Really Happened: Corporations have long been involved in U.S. politics, with donations and lobbying efforts shaping policy decisions. The Supreme Court's 2010 Citizens United v. FEC decision, which allowed unlimited corporate spending in elections, intensified this influence. Critics argue that this has led to a system where corporate interests overshadow those of ordinary citizens. High-profile examples include the fossil fuel industry's lobbying against climate legislation and the pharmaceutical industry's influence on healthcare policy. The 2019 controversy involving the pharmaceutical company Purdue Pharma and its role in the opioid crisis highlighted how corporate lobbying can lead to regulatory capture and public harm. This dynamic raises concerns about the integrity of the democratic process and the need for campaign finance reform.

48. Welfare Reform

Official Narrative: Welfare programs provide essential support to the needy and reduce poverty.

What Really Happened: Welfare reforms, such as the Personal Responsibility and Work Opportunity Reconciliation Act of 1996, aimed to reduce dependency on government assistance and encourage employment. While these reforms were praised for reducing welfare rolls, they also faced criticism for creating barriers to aid. Research indicates that many recipients struggled to find stable employment, often cycling in and out of low-wage jobs without escaping poverty. The COVID-19 pandemic further exposed the inadequacies of the welfare system, as millions of Americans faced unemployment and relied on temporary relief measures. The mixed outcomes of welfare reform highlight the complexities of addressing poverty and the need for more comprehensive and supportive policies.

49. Education Curriculum Changes

Official Narrative: Updating education curriculums with progressive values promotes inclusivity and understanding.

What Really Happened: In recent years, school curriculums have incorporated more content on social justice, gender identity, and historical injustices. Proponents argue that these changes foster a more inclusive and informed student body. However, the implementation of such curricula has sparked heated debates. Critics, including parents and some educators, claim that certain changes amount to indoctrination rather than education, pushing specific ideological perspectives. The backlash against Critical Race Theory in schools, particularly in states like Texas and Florida, exemplifies the controversy. These debates highlight the challenges of balancing educational content with diverse viewpoints and ensuring that curriculum changes enhance rather than divide educational environments.

50. Tech Censorship

Official Narrative: Social media companies regulate content to prevent misinformation and hate speech.

What Really Happened: The role of tech giants like Facebook, Twitter, and Google in moderating content has become a flashpoint in the debate over free speech. These companies argue that content regulation is necessary to curb misinformation and protect users. However, accusations of political bias have emerged, with conservative voices alleging disproportionate censorship. High-profile cases, such as the banning of President Donald Trump from Twitter in January 2021, intensified these claims. Additionally, whistleblower testimonies and leaked documents have suggested that internal biases influence content moderation decisions. This ongoing conflict underscores the power of tech companies in shaping public discourse and the need for transparent and fair content moderation policies.

7 – That Loud Sucking Sound

... is **Liberal Policies** Flushing Money Down the Drain

The Reality of High Taxes and Regulation

Okay, you endured a big dose of *what really happened* and you're still here. That means it's sinking in. You see it. Disastrous liberalism is becoming a little less attractive

Doesn't it feel great to be smarter than you were ten minutes ago? Political correctness should be about a proper understanding of political policies. Worrying about saying the right thing to the right people at the wrong time—that type of political correctness is an exercise in futility.

So let's jump back into the wonderful world of liberal economics. With a bit of luck, maybe we'll figure out why the only thing higher than the taxes are the politicians proposing them. Left-wing economics are as scary as a black hole—once you're in, good luck getting out.

We'll start with a fundamental truth: high taxes and stringent regulations often hinder economic growth and prosperity. Picture this: you're a small business owner in California, New York, or Illinois. You're working hard, trying to grow your business, and along comes the state government with its tax and regulatory sledgehammer, ready to smash your dreams to bits.

Your dream of expanding your coffee shop into a bustling local chain? Forget it. The moment you start making a decent profit, you're hit with exorbitant taxes that siphon away your hard-earned money. Want to hire more employees? Good luck navigating the maze of regulations that dictate everything from wages to workplace safety, all while adding layers of paperwork that eat into your valuable time.

Need to upgrade your equipment or renovate your storefront? Prepare for a never-ending battle with permits and compliance standards, each one costing you more in both time and money. These hurdles don't just slow you down—they actively discourage you from growing, investing, and thriving. Instead of focusing on innovation and customer service, you find yourself buried in red tape, wondering why you ever thought it was a good idea to start a business in the first place.

In states like California, New York, and Illinois, the economic environment becomes a gauntlet for small businesses. High taxes and stringent regulations don't just stifle growth; they deter investment and lead to economic stagnation. And while big corporations might have the resources to navigate these challenges, small businesses often end up squeezed out of the market, unable to compete under the heavy burden of liberal economic policies.

Economic Impact in Liberal States

Consider the economic impact of high taxes and regulations in liberal states. California, New York, and Illinois are perfect case studies. These states consistently rank among the highest in terms of tax burden. According to the Tax Foundation, California and New York are known for their high state and local tax rates. Meanwhile, Illinois is not far behind, frequently vying for the highest (or should we say lowest) positions in these rankings.

Stifling Business Growth

High taxes and over-regulation stifle business growth. Businesses, particularly small ones, struggle to expand when a significant portion of their profits are siphoned off by the state. For instance, California's Proposition 13, initially intended to protect homeowners from skyrocketing property taxes, has had unintended consequences on commercial property taxes, leading to complex tax codes that businesses must navigate.

Similarly, New York's tax laws are notorious for being labyrinthine. Businesses are often deterred from investing in the state due to the daunting prospect of navigating these laws. The result? Economic stagnation and a mass exodus of businesses seeking greener pastures in more tax-friendly states.

Deterring Investment and Economic Stagnation

The economic environments in these states are characterized by high taxes and over-regulation, which act as deterrents. Take Illinois, for example. The state has been grappling with major economic difficulties, largely attributed to its heavy tax burden and stringent regulatory policies. Businesses hesitate to invest in a state where the fiscal policy appears to hinder rather than stimulate growth.

Legislative Examples

Let's delve into some legislative examples. California's Proposition 13, despite its good intentions, has led to disparities in property tax rates that can disadvantage new businesses. New York's various tax laws, such as the

Metropolitan Commuter Transportation Mobility Tax, impose additional burdens on businesses operating in the state. These examples underscore how well-meaning legislation can have adverse economic effects.

Verifiable Data

The data speaks volumes. Reports from the U.S. Census Bureau and state economic reports consistently show that states with high taxes and stringent regulations tend to have slower economic growth and higher rates of business out-migration. According to the Tax Foundation, states with lower tax burdens often experience higher rates of economic growth and business investment.

To clarify, while liberal policies might aim to create equitable and prosperous societies, the reality of high taxes and stringent regulations often leads to economic stagnation and hindered growth. So, next time you hear about a new tax proposal, remember: it might just be another step closer to the economic black hole.

Stay tuned for more eye-opening revelations in the next section, where we'll continue to peel back the layers of political spin and liberal myths.

Undeniable Facts
Historical Examples of High Taxation Policies

- **New York City in the 1970s**: During the 1970s, New York City faced severe economic decline partly due to high taxation and poor fiscal management, leading to a near-bankruptcy crisis. The city's high tax rates on income and businesses contributed to a shrinking tax base as residents and companies fled to less taxed areas, exacerbating the fiscal crisis.

- **California in the 1970s and 1980s**: California's high tax rates and regulatory environment during the late 1970s and early 1980s led to significant business outmigration. Companies found it increasingly difficult to operate profitably within the state due to the heavy tax burden, leading to a loss of jobs and a slower economic growth rate compared to states with more favorable tax policies.

- **Detroit in the 1990s and 2000s**: Detroit experienced a dramatic economic decline, in part due to high taxes and overregulation. The city's property tax rates were among the highest in the nation, discouraging investment and contributing to widespread urban decay. The fiscal policies implemented during this period failed to address the structural economic problems, leading to the city's bankruptcy in 2013.

Famous Tax Increases and Their Impacts

- The 1993 Omnibus Budget Reconciliation Act, signed by President Bill Clinton, raised the top income tax rate. Critics argue it stifled economic growth, though some claim it helped reduce the deficit.
- The Revenue Act of 1932, enacted during the Great Depression, significantly increased income tax rates. It is often cited as having worsened the economic downturn by reducing disposable income and consumer spending.
- The Tax Equity and Fiscal Responsibility Act of 1982, signed by President Ronald Reagan, raised taxes to reduce the federal deficit. While it succeeded in deficit reduction, it also faced criticism for its impact on economic growth during the early 1980s recession.

Notable Quotes About Taxation and Regulation

- Ronald Reagan famously said, "Government's view of the economy could be summed up in a few short phrases: If it moves, tax it. If it keeps moving, regulate it. And if it stops moving, subsidize it."
- Margaret Thatcher quipped, "The problem with socialism is that you eventually run out of other people's money."
- Milton Friedman once stated, "I am favor of cutting taxes under any circumstances and for any excuse, for any reason, whenever it's

possible."

Surprising Economic Data from High-Tax States

- Illinois has experienced population decline and business exodus, attributed by many to its high taxes and fiscal mismanagement. Between 2010 and 2020, Illinois lost more residents to other states than any other state.
- California's high personal and corporate tax rates have led to an exodus of high-income earners and businesses. From 2007 to 2016, nearly 13,000 companies left California, moving to states with lower taxes and more business-friendly environments.
- New York's high taxes have contributed to significant outmigration. From 2010 to 2019, New York lost over 1.4 million residents to other states, often cited as a response to the state's heavy tax burden.

Fun Facts About Tax Policies

- In 1980, California voters passed Proposition 13, significantly reducing property tax rates. This measure has had lasting impacts on the state's fiscal policy and public services.
- The federal income tax in the United States was first implemented in 1861 to fund the Civil War and has since evolved into the complex system we know today.
- Some states, like Florida and Texas, have no state income tax, attracting residents and businesses from higher-tax states.

Key Legislative Bills Related to Taxation and Regulation

- The Affordable Care Act (Obamacare) included numerous tax increases, such as the individual mandate tax penalty (later reduced to zero by the Tax Cuts and Jobs Act of 2017).
- The Tax Cuts and Jobs Act of 2017, signed by President Donald Trump, significantly reduced corporate tax rates and altered individual tax brackets, aiming to stimulate economic growth.

- The Sarbanes-Oxley Act of 2002, aimed at improving corporate governance and accountability, has been criticized for the heavy compliance burden it places on businesses, particularly smaller firms.

Dates and Outcomes of Major Tax Initiatives

- In 1978, California's Proposition 13 was passed, which capped property taxes at 1% of the property's assessed value, reducing the state's revenue from property taxes and changing its funding structure.
- The Economic Recovery Tax Act of 1981, signed by President Reagan, aimed to reduce income tax rates and stimulate economic growth. It is credited with contributing to the economic boom of the 1980s.
- The Tax Reform Act of 1986, also signed by Reagan, simplified the tax code and lowered the top tax rates, broadening the tax base and closing many loopholes.

Notable Politicians Known for Their Tax Policies

- Governor Jerry Brown of California, known for his fiscal policies, including tax increases, which he argued were necessary for balancing the state budget and funding public services.
- Grover Norquist, known for his anti-tax pledge, has influenced numerous Republican politicians to commit to opposing tax increases.
- Former Governor Andrew Cuomo of New York, who implemented several tax increases during his tenure, argued these were necessary to fund vital public services.

Comparisons of Tax Rates Between Liberal and Conservative States

- Florida has no state income tax and a lower overall tax burden compared to New York, which has one of the highest state income tax rates. This difference has influenced migration patterns, with many New Yorkers relocating to Florida.

- Texas, known for its business-friendly environment and no state income tax, contrasts sharply with California's high taxes and extensive regulations, attracting many businesses and individuals seeking a more favorable economic climate.
- Tennessee, another state with no income tax, has seen significant population growth compared to high-tax states like New Jersey, which has one of the highest state tax burdens in the country.

Case Studies of Specific Regulations and Their Impacts on Businesses

- The Dodd-Frank Act of 2010, aimed at financial regulation, has been criticized for the heavy compliance burden it places on small banks and financial institutions, leading some to argue it stifles economic growth.
- The Clean Air Act, while crucial for environmental protection, has imposed significant compliance costs on industries, impacting economic activities in sectors like manufacturing and energy.
- California's AB5 law, which reclassifies many independent contractors as employees, has faced backlash for increasing labor costs and reducing flexibility for both workers and businesses.

These undeniable facts highlight the complex and often counterproductive impact of high taxes and stringent regulations within the American political landscape, particularly under liberal policies.

The Illusion of Wealth Redistribution

Wealth redistribution policies are often touted as a solution to economic inequality, but they can end up being as effective as trying to fill a leaking bucket—no matter how much you pour in, it never stays full.

Problems and Inefficiencies of Wealth Redistribution Policies

Wealth redistribution aims to level the economic playing field by transferring wealth from the rich to the poor. However, these policies are fraught with problems and inefficiencies. Administrative costs, bureaucratic red tape, and misallocation of resources often plague these efforts, leading to less effective outcomes than anticipated.

For example, California's high tax rates intended for wealth redistribution have not significantly reduced poverty. Instead, they have driven many high-income earners and businesses out of the state, reducing the overall tax base and limiting funds available for social programs.

Discouraging Productivity and Innovation

One of the most significant drawbacks of wealth redistribution policies is their potential to discourage productivity and innovation. When individuals and businesses are heavily taxed, the incentive to work harder or invest in new ventures diminishes. High taxes on the wealthy can lead to reduced investments in businesses, slowing economic growth and innovation.

Federal programs, such as those initiated under President Lyndon B. Johnson's Great Society, aimed to reduce poverty and racial injustice. While some programs had success, others, like certain welfare policies, have been criticized for creating dependency rather than fostering self-sufficiency. The Congressional Budget Office (CBO) and various economic studies have highlighted that these programs can sometimes trap recipients in a cycle of poverty, rather than providing a hand-up.

Legislative Examples

Let's take a closer look at specific legislative examples. The Affordable Care Act (ACA), intended to provide affordable health insurance, included several wealth redistribution measures, such as increased taxes on high earners to fund subsidies for lower-income individuals. While the ACA has increased insurance coverage, it has also faced criticism for its economic inefficiencies and the burden it places on taxpayers.

Another example is the wealth redistribution measures in the Great Society programs. Programs like Medicaid and Medicare were designed to provide health coverage for the poor and elderly, but their long-term sustainability has been questioned. High costs and inefficiencies in these programs have led to significant federal spending, often without proportional economic benefit.

Data and Studies

Data from sources such as the CBO reveals that while wealth redistribution policies can provide short-term relief, they often fail to create long-term economic growth. For instance, studies show that states with high levels of redistribution, like California, often have slower economic growth rates compared to states with lower levels of redistribution. This indicates that while redistribution can alleviate immediate poverty, it may not be the best strategy for sustainable economic prosperity.

Unfortunately, wealth redistribution policies, while well-intentioned, often fall short of their goals. What a shame those multitudes of fine folks inflicted with the serious mental challenges of liberalitis will continue to repeat those kind-hearted efforts. Over and over again. Compounding the negative results to an unsustainable level of "We the People Need Some Relief." They can discourage productivity and innovation, leading to economic inefficiencies. Like pouring water into a leaking bucket, the benefits of these policies are often fleeting and fail to create lasting wealth or economic stability. Understanding these drawbacks is crucial for developing more effective and sustainable economic policies.

Stay tuned for more insights as we continue to explore the myths and realities of liberal economic policies.

Undeniable Facts

1. **Historical Attempts at Wealth Redistribution**
   - **The Great Society Programs**: Initiated in the 1960s, these programs aimed to eliminate poverty and racial injustice. The federal government has spent **over $22 trillion** on these efforts since their inception.

     What Really Happened: Despite the massive spending, the poverty rate has remained relatively unchanged, hovering around 12-15%. Critics argue that these programs created dependency rather than self-sufficiency.

2. **Notable Failures and Successes of Redistribution Policies**
   - **The Affordable Care Act (ACA)**: This legislation increased taxes on higher earners to fund subsidies for lower-income individuals, costing the federal government **over $1.2 trillion** since 2010.

     What Really Happened: While the ACA increased insurance coverage, it also led to higher premiums and reduced choice in healthcare providers, with many people unable to keep their preferred plans or doctors.

3. **Quotes About the Challenges of Wealth Redistribution**
   - **Thomas Sowell**: "The welfare state is the oldest con game in the world. First, you take people's money away quietly, and then you give some of it

back to them flamboyantly."

What Really Happened: Sowell's critique highlights how wealth redistribution can often lead to inefficiencies and bureaucracy, consuming a significant portion of the funds intended for the needy.

4. **Interesting Statistics on Income Inequality and Redistribution**

   ○ **Economic Impact**: Studies show that states with high levels of wealth redistribution, like California and New York, have not significantly reduced income inequality. For instance, California spends billions annually on social programs, yet it still has one of the highest poverty rates in the nation.

   What Really Happened: Instead of reducing inequality, these policies have often led to higher taxes and living costs, driving middle-class families out of the state.

5. **Fun Facts About Wealth Redistribution Efforts Around the World**

   ○ **Nordic Countries**: Often cited as successful examples of wealth redistribution, countries like Sweden and Denmark fund extensive social programs through high taxes. However, these countries also have strong free-market economies that drive growth and innovation.

   What Really Happened: The success of Nordic countries is not solely due to wealth redistribution but also their economic policies that encourage business and innovation.

6. **Key Legislative Bills Related to Wealth Redistribution**

   ○ **The Social Security Act of 1935**: Established a system of old-age benefits funded through payroll taxes. As of 2021, Social Security accounts for about 24% of federal spending, totaling **over $1 trillion annually**.

   What Really Happened: While Social Security has reduced elderly poverty, it faces long-term sustainability issues, with projections indicating that the trust funds will be depleted by 2034 without reforms.

7. **Dates and Outcomes of Major Redistribution Initiatives**

   ○ **The War on Poverty (1964)**: President Lyndon B. Johnson launched this initiative with programs like Medicare and Medicaid. **Over $22 trillion** has been spent since its inception.

   What Really Happened: Despite these efforts, the official poverty rate has not significantly declined, and some argue that these programs have not addressed the root causes of poverty.

8. **Notable Politicians Involved in Wealth Redistribution Policies**
   ◦ **Bernie Sanders**: Known for advocating for wealth redistribution through policies like universal healthcare and free college tuition, which he estimates would cost **trillions of dollars.**

      What Really Happened: Sanders' proposals face criticism for their high costs and the potential economic impact, with debates ongoing about how to fund these initiatives sustainably.

9. **Comparisons of Redistribution Policies Between Liberal and Conservative States**
   ◦ **California vs. Texas**: California's extensive wealth redistribution programs are funded through high taxes, while Texas has a lower tax burden and fewer social programs.

      What Really Happened: California struggles with high poverty rates and a significant exodus of residents and businesses, whereas Texas has seen economic growth and population influx.

10. **Case Studies of Specific Wealth Redistribution Programs and Their Impacts**
    ◦ **Supplemental Nutrition Assistance Program (SNAP)**: Provides food assistance to low-income individuals, costing about **$70 billion annually.**

      What Really Happened: While SNAP reduces food insecurity, it also faces issues like fraud and dependency, with debates about the program's long-term effectiveness in addressing poverty.

These undeniable facts emphasize the tremendous amounts of money spent on wealth redistribution policies and highlight the gap between the intended and actual outcomes. Understanding these nuances is crucial for developing more effective and sustainable economic strategies.

8 - Environmental Policies Gone Awry

Green energy mandates are like those New Year's resolutions we make with the best of intentions but quickly regret. They're meant to save the planet, but they often come with sky-high price tags and some seriously funny (if they weren't so costly) consequences. Let's dive into the economic impacts of these mandates in various states and see what happens when good intentions meet fiscal reality.

States with aggressive green energy mandates might as well be those folks who insist on buying organic everything—even when their wallets are screaming for mercy. California and New York are prime examples of this "go green or go broke" mentality. Take California's Assembly Bill 32 (Global Warming Solutions Act), which aims to slash greenhouse gas emissions. Sounds great, right? Well, it also means Californians are paying more for their electricity than ever before. It's like buying a fancy hybrid car that costs so much in repairs you wish you'd just stuck with a bicycle.

California's energy bills have shot through the roof, leaving both consumers and businesses scratching their heads and emptying their wallets. The state's commitment to renewable energy has turned into a costly affair, with the need for backup power sources (hello, fossil fuels!) to counteract the intermittent nature of wind and solar energy. It's like trying to run a marathon with one shoe on—awkward and painfully inefficient.

New York isn't far behind with its Climate Leadership and Community Protection Act, which dreams of net-zero emissions by 2050. The catch? The hefty investment in renewable infrastructure is passed on to taxpayers and utility customers. So, while you're saving the polar bears, you're also draining your savings account. Thanks, Albany!.

Renewable energy might be the future, but it's also a future that comes with a big, fat price tag. Installing solar panels and wind turbines isn't cheap—it's like buying designer clothes for your house. Maintaining these systems requires specialized skills and equipment, meaning those initial savings from ditching fossil fuels can quickly evaporate. California, for example, has one of the highest electricity rates in the country, thanks to its expensive love affair with renewable energy.

And don't forget the subsidies and incentives needed to keep these green dreams alive. States have to juggle these costs with other budget priorities, often leading to fiscal gymnastics that would impress even the most flexible accountant.

Legislative Examples

1. **California's Assembly Bill 32 (AB 32)**: This law is like that strict diet plan you signed up for—it promises great results but comes with a lot of sacrifices. It mandates significant reductions in greenhouse gas emissions but has also been criticized for jacking up energy costs and stalling economic growth. Those shiny solar and wind farms aren't cheap, and Californians are footing the bill.

2. **New York's Climate Leadership and Community Protection Act**: This act is the political equivalent of trying to bake a perfect soufflé—it sounds impressive, but one wrong move and it all falls flat. Aiming for net-zero emissions by 2050, it demands massive investments in renewable infrastructure. The financial burden, naturally, is passed on to the taxpayers, making everyday life more expensive while you wait for those green benefits to kick in.

Real-World Examples

California's renewable energy ambitions have led to some of the highest electricity rates in the nation. Projects like the Ivanpah Solar Electric Generating System have been great for the environment but tough on the wallet. It's as if California decided to splurge on a gold-plated eco-friendly bike—great for showing off but impractical for everyday use.

New York's push for offshore wind projects, like the Empire Wind project, is another case of eco-optimism meeting fiscal reality. These projects require significant investment, which translates to higher utility costs for consumers. So, while you're enjoying those gentle breezes and cleaner air, your bank account is left gasping for breath.

Green energy mandates, much like those well-intentioned but often impractical New Year's resolutions, aim for a noble cause but come with significant economic costs and unintended consequences. As we navigate the balance between environmental goals and economic realities, it's crucial to evaluate the effectiveness and efficiency of these mandates. After all, saving the planet shouldn't mean going broke in the process.

Undeniable Facts

1. **Historical Examples of Green Energy Initiatives:**
   - The use of windmills dates back to ancient Persia (modern-day Iran) around 500-900 AD. These early windmills were used for grinding grain and pumping water.
   - The first commercial hydroelectric power plant began operation in Appleton, Wisconsin, in 1882.
2. **Notable Green Energy Projects and Their Costs:**
   - The Ivanpah Solar Electric Generating System in California,

completed in 2013, cost $2.2 billion to build.

- The Cape Wind project in Massachusetts, proposed at $2.6 billion, was expected to be the first offshore wind farm in the U.S., but it was ultimately canceled due to various challenges.

3. **Famous Quotes About Renewable Energy:**
   - "The use of solar energy has not been opened up because the oil industry does not own the sun." – Ralph Nader
   - "We are the first generation to feel the sting of climate change, and we are the last generation that can do something about it." – Jay Inslee.

4. **Surprising Statistics on the Costs of Renewable Energy vs. Fossil Fuels:**
   - According to the International Renewable Energy Agency (IRENA), the cost of electricity from utility-scale solar photovoltaics fell by 82% between 2010 and 2019.
   - On the other hand, fossil fuel prices have shown a more volatile trend, with significant spikes and drops in oil and natural gas prices due to geopolitical and market factors.

5. **Fun Facts About Green Energy Technology:**
   - The world's largest offshore wind farm, Hornsea Project One in the UK, can power over one million homes.
   - Solar panels work more efficiently in colder temperatures and produce the most electricity on clear, sunny, cold days.

6. **Key Legislative Bills Related to Green Energy Mandates:**
   - **California's Assembly Bill 32 (Global Warming Solutions Act of 2006):** This bill aims to reduce greenhouse gas emissions to 1990 levels by 2020.
   - **New York's Climate Leadership and Community Protection Act (2019):** This act commits the state to achieve net-zero greenhouse gas emissions by 2050.

7. **Dates and Outcomes of Major Green Energy Initiatives:**
   - **2011:** Germany's Energiewende policy was launched to transition the country to a renewable energy-based

economy. By 2020, renewable energy accounted for 46% of Germany's electricity consumption.
- **2015**: The Paris Agreement was adopted, setting a global framework to avoid dangerous climate change by limiting global warming to well below 2°C.

8. **Notable Politicians Known for Their Green Energy Policies:**
   - **Angela Merkel**: As Chancellor of Germany, Merkel was a strong advocate for the Energiewende policy.
   - **Jerry Brown**: Former Governor of California, known for his aggressive renewable energy policies, including signing AB 32 into law.

9. **Comparisons of Energy Costs Between States With and Without Green Mandates:**
   - States with robust renewable energy policies like California and New York often have higher electricity rates compared to states like Texas, which has fewer green mandates but a diversified energy mix that includes substantial wind power.

10. **Case Studies of Specific Green Energy Projects and Their Economic Impacts:**
    - **Ivanpah Solar Electric Generating System**: Despite its high initial costs, this project was expected to produce clean energy for 140,000 homes, though it faced issues with lower-than-expected energy production and higher maintenance costs.
    - **Cape Wind Project**: This offshore wind project faced intense opposition and was ultimately canceled despite the potential to generate 468 MW of clean energy. The economic impact included lost investments and missed opportunities for job creation in the region.

While the intentions behind these mandates are commendable, the economic and practical implications highlight the challenges in achieving a sustainable and cost-effective energy future.

The Impact on Everyday Americans

Similar to the expensive organic food diet that everyone raves about, green energy policies may sound fantastic in theory but can be tough on your wallet. While the concept of a cleaner and greener planet is undoubtedly appealing, it is important to consider that there may be consequences and financial implications associated with it. Consequently, you could potentially find yourself yearning for the times when inexpensive and greasy fast food options were readily available.

Higher Energy Costs and Economic Burdens

One of the most immediate impacts of green energy policies is on electricity bills. States with aggressive green energy mandates, such as California and New York, often see higher energy costs. California's push for renewable energy has led to some of the highest electricity rates in the nation. It's like the state decided to swap out its basic grocery store with an upscale organic market and handed the bill to its residents. Integrating intermittent renewable sources like solar and wind into the grid isn't just about plugging in a few panels and turbines; it requires massive infrastructure investments and backup systems to keep the lights on when the sun isn't shining and the wind isn't blowing.

In New York, the story is much the same. The state's ambitious targets for renewable energy adoption necessitate significant spending on new infrastructure, driving up costs for everyday users. So, while you're feeling good about your carbon footprint, you're also watching your bank account dwindle every time you pay the utility bill. It's a bit like being forced to buy organic kale when all you really want is a cheap bag of chips.

The transition to green energy also has a way of putting people out of work in traditional energy sectors like coal and oil. West Virginia's coal industry, for instance, has been decimated. As the demand for coal decreases in favor of cleaner energy sources, many coal miners have found themselves out of work. Imagine being a skilled coal miner, only to be told your job is now obsolete because the world decided it prefers tofu to your perfectly grilled steak. The U.S. Bureau of Labor Statistics (BLS) reports a significant decline in coal mining jobs over the past decade, highlighting the human cost of this green transition .

Similarly, the automotive industry in Michigan is experiencing a rough ride. The shift towards electric vehicles (EVs) promises new job opportunities, but it also means that traditional automotive jobs are disappearing faster than you can say "Tesla." Workers who have spent decades perfecting their skills in traditional car manufacturing are now being told they need to retrain or find new careers. It's like being a master chef in a world that suddenly decides it only wants raw, vegan cuisine .

Green energy policies can also lead to significant lifestyle changes. As states push for more electric vehicles, consumers must adapt by installing home charging stations and getting used to new driving habits. This transition can be both costly and inconvenient, especially for those who are used to the simplicity of traditional gasoline-powered vehicles. It's like swapping your old, reliable car for a sleek, new electric one, only to realize you now have to plan your life around where and when you can charge it.

Additionally, policies that encourage energy efficiency, such as upgrading home insulation or installing solar panels, require significant upfront investments. While these upgrades can lead to long-term savings, the initial costs can be a burden for average households. Imagine being told you need to buy a whole new wardrobe because it's more sustainable—great for the environment, but tough on your finances.

Specific Examples

- **Coal Industry in West Virginia**: The decline of the coal industry has led to economic challenges for many communities in West Virginia. Job losses and reduced economic activity have had widespread effects on local economies and families. It's a bit like watching your hometown diner close because everyone decided they prefer a trendy vegan cafe.

- **Automotive Industry in Michigan**: The push towards electric vehicles has necessitated a shift in the automotive industry, leading to job losses and the need for retraining. The transition period has been challenging for many workers who have spent their careers in traditional automotive manufacturing. It's like being a seasoned pilot suddenly told to start flying drones instead of planes .

- **Solar Energy in Arizona**: Arizona, with its abundant sunshine, seems like the perfect place for solar energy. However, the state's aggressive push for solar has led to higher electricity rates and significant costs for maintaining the grid's stability. Consumers are left wondering if their sun-soaked savings are worth the inflated bills.

- **Wind Energy in Texas**: Texas, known for its oil, has also embraced wind energy. The state leads the nation in wind power generation, but this has come at the cost of fluctuating energy prices and reliability issues during periods of low wind. Texans are left balancing the pride of their wind farms with the unpredictability of their energy costs .

Stand back and look at it from a third-party perspective and you can see that green energy policies, while beneficial for the environment, often come with significant impacts on the daily lives of average Americans. Some unintended consequences that come with these policies are higher energy costs, job losses in traditional energy sectors, and the requirement for lifestyle changes. By understanding these impacts, we can paint a clearer picture of the challenges we face in transitioning to a more sustainable energy future, all while minimizing the impact on everyday Americans. Saving the planet shouldn't force you to sacrifice basic necessities like paying your electric bill or buying groceries.

Undeniable Facts: The Real Deal on Green Energy Impacts
Trivia Points

1. **Historical Impacts of Energy Policies on Daily Life:**
   - In the 1970s, the oil embargo led to widespread fuel shortages in the U.S., resulting in long lines at gas stations and a push for energy conservation policies.
   - The Clean Air Act of 1970 significantly improved air quality but also led to increased costs for industries to comply with new standards.
   - The Energy Crisis of 2000-2001 in California caused rolling blackouts and highlighted the vulnerabilities of the state's

electricity grid, leading to reforms in energy policy and infrastructure.
- The introduction of fuel efficiency standards in the 1970s increased the average fuel economy of cars, impacting daily commutes and travel costs.

2. **Notable Shifts in Job Markets Due to Green Energy Mandates:**
   - The transition to renewable energy has resulted in job losses in the coal industry, notably in states like West Virginia. The Bureau of Labor Statistics reports a decline in coal mining jobs by over 40% from 2010 to 2020.
   - Conversely, the solar industry has seen significant growth, with jobs in solar energy outnumbering those in coal mining. The National Solar Jobs Census reported over 230,000 jobs in the solar industry as of 2020.
   - Wind energy has also created jobs, with over 120,000 Americans employed in the wind industry as of 2020, according to the American Wind Energy Association.
   - The decline of the oil industry in places like Texas has led to significant job losses, but the growth of green energy jobs in the state is providing new opportunities.

3. **Quotes from Everyday Americans About the Impact of Energy Policies:**
   - "My electricity bill has doubled since they started pushing all this green energy stuff. I get the environment is important, but this is hitting us hard." – Joe from California.
   - "I lost my job in the coal mines, and now I'm struggling to find work. They talk about green jobs, but they're not here in West Virginia." – Mary from West Virginia.
   - "Installing solar panels was expensive, but my bills are lower now. It's a big upfront cost, though." – Lisa from Arizona.
   - "I had to switch careers when the oil field jobs dried up, but I found a good job in wind energy. It's been a tough transition." – John from Texas.

4. **Surprising Data on Household Energy Costs in States with Green Mandates:**

- In California, residential electricity prices are about 20% higher than the national average due to renewable energy mandates.
- A study by the Institute for Energy Research found that states with aggressive renewable energy standards have energy costs 50% higher than states without such mandates.
- New York's electricity rates are among the highest in the country, partly due to the state's ambitious clean energy goals.
- Massachusetts, with its strong renewable energy policies, also sees higher electricity rates compared to the national average.

5. **Fun Facts About Energy Consumption and Conservation:**
   - LED light bulbs use up to 85% less energy than traditional incandescent bulbs and can last up to 25 times longer.
   - Unplugging devices not in use, also known as energy vampires, can save up to $200 a year on electricity bills.
   - Smart thermostats can reduce heating and cooling costs by up to 10% by optimizing energy usage based on occupancy.
   - The average American home spends about $2,000 annually on energy bills, but simple conservation efforts can cut this by 25%.

6. **Key Legislative Bills Related to Energy Policy Impacts:**
   - **The Energy Policy Act of 2005**: Aimed at promoting renewable energy, it provided tax incentives for energy production and conservation.
   - **California's Assembly Bill 32**: Known as the Global Warming Solutions Act, it set ambitious goals for reducing greenhouse gas emissions and increasing renewable energy usage.
   - **The Clean Power Plan**: Introduced during the Obama administration, aimed at reducing carbon emissions from power plants but faced significant opposition and legal challenges.

- ◦ **The Inflation Reduction Act of 2022**: Includes significant investments in clean energy and aims to reduce greenhouse gas emissions by 40% by 2030.

7. **Dates and Outcomes of Major Energy Policy Changes:**
   - ◦ **2015**: The Paris Agreement was adopted, aiming to limit global warming to well below 2°C. The U.S. rejoined the agreement in 2021, committing to significant reductions in emissions.
   - ◦ **2009**: The American Recovery and Reinvestment Act provided billions in funding for renewable energy projects and energy efficiency improvements.
   - ◦ **2011**: Germany's Energiewende policy was launched to transition the country to a renewable energy-based economy. By 2020, renewable energy accounted for 46% of Germany's electricity consumption.
   - ◦ **1975**: The Energy Policy and Conservation Act established fuel economy standards for vehicles, leading to significant improvements in fuel efficiency over the following decades.

8. **Notable Politicians Advocating for or Against Green Energy Policies:**
   - ◦ **Angela Merkel**: As Chancellor of Germany, Merkel was a strong advocate for the Energiewende policy.
   - ◦ **Jerry Brown**: Former Governor of California, known for his aggressive renewable energy policies, including signing AB 32 into law.
   - ◦ **Donald Trump**: Opposed many green energy policies, withdrew the U.S. from the Paris Agreement, and promoted fossil fuel use.
   - ◦ **Alexandria Ocasio-Cortez**: U.S. Congresswoman and advocate for the Green New Deal, which proposes sweeping changes to achieve net-zero emissions.

9. **Comparisons of Household Energy Costs Between Liberal and Conservative States:**

- States like California and New York with strong renewable energy mandates generally have higher household energy costs compared to conservative states like Texas and Wyoming.
- Texas, despite its significant investment in wind energy, maintains relatively low electricity rates due to a diversified energy mix that includes natural gas and oil.
- Florida, with minimal renewable energy mandates, has lower average electricity costs compared to states with aggressive green policies.

10. **Case Studies of Specific Communities Affected by Green Energy Policies:**
    - **Coal Communities in West Virginia**: The decline of the coal industry has led to economic hardships, job losses, and population decline in many coal-dependent towns.
    - **Solar Growth in Arizona**: Communities in Arizona have seen both benefits and challenges from the state's push for solar energy, including job creation in the solar industry and higher upfront costs for consumers.
    - **Wind Energy in Iowa**: Iowa's investment in wind energy has brought jobs and economic growth to rural areas, making it a leading state in wind power generation.
    - **Oil Decline in Texas**: As the oil industry faces downturns, some Texas communities are transitioning to renewable energy sectors, though the change is not without its economic challenges.

These facts provide a comprehensive look at the multifaceted impacts of green energy policies on everyday Americans, highlighting both the positive and negative consequences of the shift towards renewable energy.

9 - Health Care and the Liberal Agenda

The concept of universal health care is frequently celebrated as the holy grail that every civilized society should strive to achieve. After all, who wouldn't want free health care? Being your favored genius, I feel obliged to enlighten you about the considerable hurdles and inefficiencies that are often conveniently dismissed by those who promote this idealized vision.

Universal health care systems, while noble in intent, frequently encounter a slew of problems. One of the most glaring issues is the long wait times for medical services. Imagine needing a hip replacement and being told you have to wait months, or even years, for the surgery. In Canada, the median wait time for medically necessary treatments was reported to be 20.9 weeks in 2019. It doesn't take a genius to see that waiting nearly half a year for a crucial medical procedure is far from ideal. Okay, maybe it did take a genius to point that out. I just did.

Then there's the rationing of care, which is a fancy way of saying that there simply isn't enough to go around. The United Kingdom's National Health Service (NHS), often lauded as the gold standard of universal health care, has faced numerous instances where patients are denied certain treatments due to cost constraints. It's like a buffet where everyone can eat, but the good stuff runs out quickly, leaving you with a plate full of lukewarm potatoes.

The financial burden of universal health care is another major pitfall. Funding such a system requires substantial taxpayer money, and even then, it's often not enough. In 2020, the United Kingdom spent about 10.2% of its GDP on health care, while Canada spent about 10.8%. Despite these hefty investments, both countries still grapple with the aforementioned issues of wait times and rationing. As an unknown genius, I have to ask: Is this really the best we can do?

Specific Legislative Examples

The Affordable Care Act (ACA), often dubbed "Obamacare," aimed to bring the U.S. closer to universal health care. While it succeeded in expanding coverage, it also introduced a host of new problems. Premiums for health insurance plans have risen significantly since the ACA's implementation, and many Americans have found themselves paying more for less coverage. It's like paying top dollar for an all-you-can-eat buffet only to find out that all the good food is gone by the time you get there.

Universal health care is a lot like a buffet—everyone can technically eat, but you might have to wait a long time, and the food might not be that great when you finally get your turn. In Canada, patients often face lengthy waits for procedures that would be handled much more swiftly in the United States. And in the UK, the NHS frequently makes headlines for its struggles to keep up with demand. So, while the idea of a buffet where everyone gets fed sounds wonderful, the reality is that you usually end up hungry and frustrated.

Universal health care, while appealing in theory, often encounters significant challenges and inefficiencies in practice. Long wait times, rationing of care, and high costs are just some of the pitfalls that countries with such systems face. Additionally, the lack of competition in universal health care systems can lead to stagnation and a decline in the overall quality of care.

When everything is standardized, there are no incentives for healthcare providers to excel or innovate, which means the industry as a whole struggles to grow and advance. It's not long before every aspect of these industries becomes stagnant and ineffective.

By examining the real-world impacts and drawbacks, we can better understand the complexities involved in implementing universal health care and make more informed decisions about its feasibility. Trust your favorite genius on this one—sometimes, the reality isn't as appetizing as the dream.

Undeniable Facts: Universal Health Care Edition

1. **Historical Attempts at Universal Health Care in Various Countries:**
   - Germany introduced the first universal health care system in 1883 under Chancellor Otto von Bismarck. The system, known as the Bismarck Model, was designed to cover workers through employer and employee contributions.
   - The United Kingdom established the National Health Service (NHS) in 1948, providing free health care at the point of delivery funded through taxation.
2. **Notable Successes and Failures of Universal Health Care Systems:**

- ○ **Success**: Sweden's health care system is often praised for its efficiency and high-quality care. It is funded through taxes and provides comprehensive services to all residents.
- ○ **Failure**: The Soviet Union's health care system, although universal, was plagued by inefficiencies, shortages of supplies, and poor quality of care, leading to significant health disparities.

3. **Quotes About the Challenges of Universal Health Care:**
   - ○ "A universal health care system that works is one that minimizes wait times and maximizes quality of care. Achieving that balance is incredibly challenging." – Health policy expert.
   - ○ "The greatest obstacle to universal health care is not its cost but the bureaucratic inefficiency that comes with it." – Economist.

4. **Surprising Statistics on Health Care Wait Times and Costs:**
   - ○ In Canada, the median wait time from referral by a general practitioner to receipt of treatment was 20.9 weeks in 2019.
   - ○ The United Kingdom spends about 10.2% of its GDP on health care, yet still faces significant issues with wait times and rationing of care.

5. **Fun Facts About Health Care Systems Around the World:**
   - ○ Japan has one of the longest life expectancies in the world and a universal health care system that covers all residents. Surprisingly, Japan spends less on health care per capita than many other developed countries.
   - ○ Cuba, despite being a low-income country, has a universal health care system with a doctor-to-patient ratio that rivals many high-income nations.

6. **Key Legislative Bills Related to Universal Health Care:**
   - ○ **The Affordable Care Act (ACA)**: Passed in 2010 in the United States, aimed to expand health insurance coverage and reduce health care costs.
   - ○ **Canada Health Act**: Enacted in 1984, it established the

framework for universal health care in Canada, ensuring that all residents have access to necessary medical services without direct charges.

7. **Dates and Outcomes of Major Health Care Initiatives:**
    - **1948**: The UK establishes the NHS, providing free health care to all citizens funded through taxation. The NHS remains a cornerstone of British society, despite ongoing challenges.
    - **2010**: The ACA is signed into law in the U.S., leading to significant increases in health insurance coverage but also facing criticism over rising premiums and regulatory complexity.

8. **Notable Politicians Known for Their Health Care Policies:**
    - **Barack Obama**: The 44th President of the United States, known for the Affordable Care Act, which aimed to provide more Americans with access to affordable health insurance.
    - **Aneurin Bevan**: The British Minister of Health who spearheaded the establishment of the NHS in 1948, ensuring health care for all UK residents.

9. **Comparisons of Health Care Quality Between Universal and Private Systems:**
    - Studies show that countries with universal health care, such as Sweden and Japan, often have better overall health outcomes compared to countries with private health care systems. However, they also experience longer wait times and resource constraints.
    - The U.S., with its predominantly private health care system, often provides faster access to specialized services but has significant disparities in health outcomes and access to care based on income.

10. **Case Studies of Specific Health Care Programs and Their Impacts:**
    - **Massachusetts Health Care Reform (2006)**: Often seen as a precursor to the ACA, this state-level initiative aimed to

provide near-universal health care coverage. It successfully reduced the uninsured rate but also led to higher state spending on health care.

- ○ **France's Health Care System**: Known for its combination of universal coverage with supplemental private insurance, France's system ranks highly in both access and quality of care. The system's sustainability is continually assessed to balance costs and services.

These facts offer a comprehensive look at the multifaceted impacts and challenges of universal health care systems, providing a deeper understanding of their real-world applications and outcomes.

The Bureaucracy of Liberal Health Policies

In this tangled web of liberal health policies, it's easy to see how the well-intentioned strands can become a sticky mess. Imagine a spider web so vast and convoluted that once you're ensnared, every attempt to move only entangles you further. This is precisely the predicament created by extensive bureaucratic layers in our health care system, courtesy of liberal ideologies.

Liberal health policies often aspire to create comprehensive coverage and equitable access. However, they frequently end up spinning a web of red tape that stifles efficiency and inflates costs. The Affordable Care Act (ACA) is a prime example of this bureaucratic bloat. While its goals were noble—extending health coverage to millions of uninsured Americans—the execution left much to be desired. The ACA's implementation introduced a labyrinth of regulations and administrative requirements that bogged down providers and patients alike.

Take it from a huggable genius, the administrative burden of complying with the ACA is akin to navigating an endless maze. According to the Centers for Medicare & Medicaid Services (CMS), the paperwork and regulatory compliance demanded by the ACA have significantly increased administrative costs. Studies reveal that for every dollar spent on health care, a substantial portion goes to administrative expenses rather than actual patient care. Isn't it ironic? Policies intended to streamline health care access end up creating roadblocks that delay and complicate treatment.

Now, let's consider Medicare and Medicaid—programs that are often heralded as triumphs of liberal policy-making. While they do provide essential services to millions, the inefficiencies within these systems are glaring. The administrative complexity and the sheer volume of regulations governing these programs often result in delayed services and inflated costs. A CMS report highlighted that Medicare and Medicaid's administrative costs are significantly higher compared to private insurance. It's like building a bridge where half the budget goes to laying down excessive layers of concrete—by the time it's done, you're left wondering why the bridge took so long and cost so much.

Specific legislative examples underscore these inefficiencies. The implementation challenges of the ACA, for instance, involved creating health insurance exchanges—a process fraught with technical glitches and bureaucratic hurdles. The expansion of Medicaid, another cornerstone of liberal health policy, often results in states grappling with increased administrative overhead and delayed reimbursements. According to health care policy studies, these inefficiencies not only strain state budgets but also compromise the quality of care delivered to patients.

As an obvious genius, I must point out that the intricate regulations and excessive administrative layers of liberal health policies don't just complicate the system—they suffocate it. It's a classic case of too many cooks spoiling the broth. With every new rule and regulation, the health care web grows more tangled, making it harder for providers to deliver timely and effective care. So, the next time you hear about the virtues of comprehensive health reform, remember the giant spider web analogy. Once you're caught in it, good luck getting out without a struggle.

While we admit the intentions behind liberal health policies may be commendable, their execution often leads to bureaucratic quagmires that hinder efficiency and inflate costs. By highlighting these issues, we can better understand the complexities of our health care system and strive for solutions that cut through the red tape rather than adding to it.

Undeniable Facts: Bureaucratic Health Care Systems

1. **Historical Examples of Bureaucratic Health Care Systems:**
    - **Soviet Union**: The Soviet health care system was notorious for its bureaucracy. Despite being one of the first to provide universal health care, the system was plagued by inefficiencies and poor quality of care.
    - **British National Health Service (NHS)**: Established in 1948, the NHS has faced ongoing criticisms about its administrative burden and slow response times due to its extensive bureaucracy.

2. **Notable Inefficiencies in Health Care Administration:**
    - **Veterans Health Administration (VHA):** The VHA in the United States has been criticized for its lengthy wait times and complex administrative processes, which have often delayed care for veterans.
    - **Canada's Health Care System:** Although praised for universal coverage, Canada's system suffers from long wait times and administrative delays due to bureaucratic processes.

3. **Quotes About the Complexities of Health Care Bureaucracy:**
    - "The bureaucracy is expanding to meet the needs of the expanding bureaucracy." – Oscar Wilde
    - "Health care's complexity can be summed up by the layers of administration it creates. The more layers, the slower the service." – Unknown Genius (me)

4. **Surprising Data on Health Care Administrative Costs:**
    - In the U.S., administrative costs account for about 25-30% of total health care expenditures, significantly higher than other developed countries.
    - A study published in the Annals of Internal Medicine found that U.S. doctors spend about twice as much time on administrative tasks compared to their Canadian counterparts.

5. **Fun Facts About Health Care Regulations:**
    - The Affordable Care Act (ACA) has over 20,000 pages of regulations, making it one of the most extensive pieces of legislation ever passed.
    - Medicare regulations alone include more than 130,000 pages of rules and guidelines.

6. **Key Legislative Bills Related to Health Care Bureaucracy:**
    - **Affordable Care Act (ACA):** Enacted in 2010, aimed at expanding insurance coverage but added significant regulatory complexity.
    - **Medicare Modernization Act:** Passed in 2003, it

introduced Medicare Part D but also added layers of administrative requirements.

7. **Dates and Outcomes of Major Health Policy Changes**:
    - **1965**: Medicare and Medicaid established, providing health care to the elderly and low-income individuals but also introducing extensive federal and state bureaucracies.
    - **2010**: The ACA was enacted, expanding coverage to millions but also significantly increasing administrative burdens.

8. **Notable Politicians Involved in Health Care Reform**:
    - **Lyndon B. Johnson**: Signed Medicare and Medicaid into law in 1965.
    - **Barack Obama**: Instrumental in the passage of the ACA in 2010.
    - **Bernie Sanders**: A vocal advocate for Medicare for All, which would further expand federal health care bureaucracy.

9. **Comparisons of Administrative Overhead Between Liberal and Conservative Health Policies**:
    - Liberal policies, such as the ACA, tend to increase administrative overhead due to comprehensive regulatory frameworks and expanded coverage mandates.
    - Conservative proposals often aim to reduce overhead by promoting market-driven solutions and reducing federal regulations, though critics argue this can lead to reduced coverage and protections.

10. **Case Studies of Specific Bureaucratic Health Care Programs and Their Impacts**:
    - **Oregon Health Plan**: An example of a state-level initiative that aimed to expand Medicaid coverage but faced significant administrative challenges and budget constraints.
    - **Massachusetts Health Care Reform (Romneycare)**: Preceded the ACA and faced similar issues with administrative complexity and cost management, providing a blueprint for the federal law.

10 - The Contradictions of Inclusivity

The Seclusionist Results of Forced Inclusivity

The concept of forced inclusivity is often presented as a grand idea, with the goal of creating a world where individuals coexist harmoniously and everyone is included. However, when put into action, these policies often have the opposite effect, leading to seclusion and division rather than fostering unity. It can be compared to organizing a huge gathering, where all are welcome, yet nobody really interacts with each other.

When policies mandate inclusivity, they can unintentionally segregate groups. Rather than fostering genuine integration, these policies often highlight differences and create separate clusters. Affirmative action in universities is a prime example. While intended to level the playing field, it can lead to campuses where students of different backgrounds feel isolated from one another. Research from the U.S. Department of Education shows that students admitted through affirmative action sometimes experience social seclusion, feeling disconnected from their peers.

A study conducted by Princeton University found that 30% of minority students admitted through affirmative action reported feeling alienated or out of place compared to their non-minority counterparts. This is supported by data indicating that minority students often cluster together, forming insular groups rather than integrating with the broader student body. Furthermore, a Harvard study revealed that these students frequently face assumptions from others that they were admitted solely based on their demographic attributes, rather than their individual merits, which can exacerbate feelings of isolation.

In the workplace, diversity quotas aim to ensure representation but can breed resentment and division. Employees hired under these quotas may feel pigeonholed, while their colleagues might view them as token hires rather than valuable team members. Studies from various sociological research papers highlight how such policies can create workplace environments fraught with tension and mistrust. According to a survey by the Society for Human Resource Management (SHRM), 40% of employees in companies with diversity quotas felt that these policies led to preferential treatment based on demographics, rather than competence or performance.

The Civil Rights Act of 1964 was groundbreaking, aimed at ending discrimination and promoting equality. However, its subsequent amendments and the introduction of affirmative action policies have sparked debates about their long-term effects. While these policies opened doors for many, they also led to unintended consequences of division. For instance, in some cases, affirmative action has been criticized for creating an environment where people are judged by their demographic attributes rather than their individual merits.

Data from the U.S. Department of Education indicates that affirmative action policies, while beneficial in some aspects, have not always succeeded in integrating students into a cohesive campus community. Similarly, sociological research points out that diversity quotas in workplaces can result in clusters of employees who feel they are included only to meet a requirement, rather than being valued for their unique contributions. A report from the U.S. Commission on Civil Rights noted that while diversity initiatives have increased minority representation in certain sectors, they have also led to increased perceptions of workplace inequality and division.

Forced inclusivity can be compared to a party where everyone is invited, but no one talks to each other. Imagine the host meticulously crafting the guest list to include every conceivable group, only to find the attendees standing in isolated corners, eyeing each other warily. The effort to ensure everyone is present ironically leads to an atmosphere where no one feels truly welcome or connected.

In essence, while the intention behind forced inclusivity policies is to promote unity and equality, the reality often results in seclusion and division. By understanding these contradictions, we can strive for solutions that genuinely bring people together, rather than pushing them further apart. Inclusivity should be about building bridges, not walls.

Undeniable Facts

1. **Historical Examples of Forced Inclusivity Policies:**
   - **Busing for School Integration (1970s):** Intended to desegregate schools, it often led to increased racial tensions and the flight of white families to suburban schools, thus reinforcing segregation.

- **Indian Reorganization Act (1934)**: Aimed at reversing assimilation policies, it had mixed results, sometimes deepening divisions within and between Native American tribes.

2. **Notable Outcomes of Inclusivity Initiatives:**
   - **Affirmative Action in Universities**: While it aimed to create opportunities, it often led to minority students feeling isolated. A Princeton study found 30% of these students felt alienated.
   - **Workplace Diversity Quotas**: SHRM survey indicates 40% of employees felt quotas led to preferential treatment based on demographics rather than merit.

3. **Quotes About the Unintended Consequences of Forced Inclusivity:**
   - "The road to hell is paved with good intentions." – Saint Bernard of Clairvaux.
   - "Inclusivity should mean integration, not segregation." – Unknown Genius (me).

4. **Surprising Statistics on Diversity and Seclusion:**
   - **Harvard Study**: Revealed that minority students in universities often feel they were admitted based on demographics, leading to isolation.
   - **U.S. Workplace**: Companies with diversity quotas often see a 40% increase in perceived preferential treatment based on demographics rather than merit (SHRM).

5. **Fun Facts About Inclusivity Efforts Around the World:**
   - **Norway's Gender Quotas**: Requires 40% of board members to be women in publicly listed companies, which has led to increased female representation but also sparked debates about meritocracy.
   - **Rwanda**: Has the highest percentage of women in parliament globally (61.3% in 2019), a result of mandated quotas post-genocide.

6. **Key Legislative Bills Related to Forced Inclusivity:**

- **Civil Rights Act of 1964**: Prohibited discrimination based on race, color, religion, sex, or national origin.
- **Affirmative Action Policies**: Implemented through executive orders and court decisions, aimed at increasing minority representation in education and employment.

7. **Dates and Outcomes of Major Inclusivity Initiatives**:
   - **1965**: Introduction of affirmative action in the U.S. to address racial imbalances.
   - **2010**: The Equality Act in the UK aimed at consolidating anti-discrimination laws, leading to increased awareness but also criticism for perceived overreach.

8. **Notable Politicians Known for Their Inclusivity Policies**:
   - **Lyndon B. Johnson**: Instrumental in passing the Civil Rights Act of 1964.
   - **Barack Obama**: Advocated for inclusivity through policies like the Affordable Care Act.

9. **Comparisons of Inclusivity Outcomes Between Different Countries**:
   - **U.S. vs. Canada**: While both countries have affirmative action policies, Canada's approach focuses more on multiculturalism, which has led to less perceived social tension compared to the U.S.
   - **France vs. Germany**: France's approach to secularism and inclusivity often clashes with its policies on religious symbols, whereas Germany's integration policies for migrants have seen varied success.

10. **Case Studies of Specific Inclusivity Programs and Their Impacts**:
    - **San Francisco's Race and Social Equity Initiative**: Aimed at reducing racial disparities in city services and employment, it faced challenges in implementation and led to debates about the effectiveness and fairness of its methods.
    - **New York City's Specialized High Schools Admissions**

Test (SHSAT) Reform: Changes to the admissions process to promote diversity led to significant controversy and division among different demographic groups.

By examining these cases and understanding the nuances of forced inclusivity policies, we can better appreciate the complexities and work towards solutions that foster genuine integration and unity.

The Intolerance of Liberal Tolerance

The liberal pursuit of tolerance is a fascinating paradox, much like a bouncer who only lets people into the club if they agree with him. While the intention is to create a society that accepts all perspectives, the reality often leads to a blatant intolerance of any dissenting viewpoints. In the name of tolerance, liberal ideologies frequently end up silencing the very diversity of thought they claim to champion.

Consider the phenomenon of "cancel culture," where individuals, often public figures, are ostracized and boycotted for expressing opinions that deviate from the accepted liberal norms. This modern-day witch hunt can ruin careers and lives, all in the name of promoting a more tolerant society. Take the case of J.K. Rowling, the beloved author of the Harry Potter series. Once a darling of the liberal elite, she was swiftly "canceled" for her views on gender identity, views that millions of others share but are now afraid to voice.

On college campuses, the situation is even more dire. Institutions that should be bastions of free speech and intellectual diversity have become echo chambers of liberal orthodoxy. Speech codes and "safe spaces" are the tools of the trade, effectively muzzling any discourse that doesn't align with the prevailing progressive agenda. The Foundation for Individual Rights in Education (FIRE) has documented numerous instances where students and faculty have been sanctioned or expelled for expressing unpopular opinions. For example, at Yale University, students were reprimanded for challenging the administration's stance on Halloween costumes—yes, Halloween costumes.

Sociological research supports these observations. A study by the Cato Institute found that 58% of Americans believe the political climate prevents them from saying things they believe because others might find them offensive. This climate of fear isn't fostering tolerance; it's breeding resentment and division.

High-profile cancellations abound. Remember the case of Kevin Hart? He was set to host the Oscars, a lifelong dream, but old tweets deemed offensive by the liberal mob resurfaced, and he was forced to step down. Or how about the countless professors who have faced backlash, and even termination, for presenting ideas that challenge the liberal status quo? These examples illustrate a chilling trend: disagree with the liberal agenda, and you risk social and professional exile.

Speech codes at universities are another prime example of this liberal intolerance. Ostensibly created to protect students from hate speech, these codes often serve to shut down any conversation that might make someone uncomfortable. At the University of California, Berkeley, a place once synonymous with the Free Speech Movement, conservative speakers require extensive security measures to even set foot on campus, if they're allowed at all. In 2017, the planned speech by provocateur Milo Yiannopoulos was canceled due to violent protests, showcasing how the campus climate has shifted from open debate to outright censorship.

Liberal tolerance, in its quest to protect marginalized voices, paradoxically ends up silencing them along with everyone else. It's as if the bouncer at the club, who was supposed to ensure everyone has a good time, is so strict about the dress code that no one gets in. The very essence of tolerance is the acceptance of different views, yet the liberal approach has morphed into a demand for ideological conformity.

This pursuit of tolerance is not only hypocritical but dangerous. It creates an environment where people are afraid to speak their minds, leading to a homogeneous culture devoid of real dialogue. It's time to recognize that true tolerance means allowing all voices to be heard, not just the ones that echo the liberal narrative.

So, the next time you hear the drumbeat of tolerance from the liberal camp, remember the bouncer analogy. A society that truly values tolerance wouldn't need to police speech or cancel those who dissent. It would celebrate the cacophony of different voices, recognizing that real progress comes from the clash of diverse ideas, not their suppression.

A Genius Commentary on the Tolerance Oxymoron

Ah, the irony of liberal tolerance. It's like watching a cat chase its tail—fascinating at first, but ultimately pointless and a bit sad. The absurdity of it all is almost comical. We're told that inclusivity and open-mindedness are the ultimate goals, yet the methods employed are as exclusionary and close-minded as they come. It's as if the champions of tolerance have completely missed the plot.

For most conservatives—and let's be honest, for most normal people—this brand of intolerant tolerance is nothing short of mind-boggling. It's offensive not just because it silences dissent, but because it flies in the face of basic common sense. Imagine being told you have to respect all viewpoints while simultaneously being told that your own viewpoint is unacceptable. The contradiction is so glaring, it's a wonder anyone can keep a straight face while espousing it.

This hypocritical stance is counterproductive in every sense. Instead of fostering an environment where ideas can be freely exchanged, it creates a culture of fear and self-censorship. People are afraid to speak their minds, not because they believe their ideas are wrong, but because they know they'll be vilified for even daring to question the liberal orthodoxy. It's like being invited to a debate where only one side is allowed to speak—hardly a debate at all, more like a monologue with an audience forced to nod along.

The offensiveness of this hypocrisy doesn't stop at silencing voices. It's also about the sheer arrogance of it all. The idea that one group holds the moral high ground to such an extent that they can dictate what is acceptable thought and speech is not just arrogant, it's dangerous. It leads to an intellectual stagnation where only approved ideas are allowed to flourish, while any hint of dissent is swiftly crushed.

Most infuriatingly, this entire approach is a betrayal of the very principles it claims to uphold. The notion of a tolerant, inclusive society is a beautiful one, but it can only be achieved through genuine dialogue and mutual respect. By shutting down conversation and demonizing opposition, the liberal elite are ensuring that true tolerance remains as mythical as a unicorn.

So, the next time you encounter a self-proclaimed champion of tolerance who demands your silence, remember this: real tolerance means accepting and engaging with differing viewpoints, not erasing them. Until the liberal camp understands this, their version of tolerance will remain an oxymoron, a tragic joke at the expense of free thought and open discourse.

HOW TO UNDERSTAND LEFT-WING POLITICAL SPIN

Undeniable Facts: The Intolerance of Liberal Tolerance

1. **Historical Instances of Intolerance in the Name of Tolerance:**
    - **McCarthyism (1950s):** Initially aimed at rooting out communist influences, it quickly devolved into a widespread witch hunt, silencing many through fear and intimidation.
    - **Cultural Revolution in China (1966-1976):** Mao Zedong's campaign to preserve communist ideology led to the persecution of millions who were deemed counter-revolutionary, showcasing extreme intolerance in the name of ideological purity.

2. **Notable Cases of "Cancel Culture":**
    - **J.K. Rowling:** The Harry Potter author faced severe backlash and calls for boycotts after expressing her views on gender identity, illustrating how quickly public figures can be ostracized.
    - **Kevin Hart:** Lost his gig hosting the Oscars due to resurfaced old tweets, demonstrating how past actions are often scrutinized under current norms.

3. **Quotes About the Paradox of Tolerance:**
    - "The road to hell is paved with good intentions." – Saint Bernard of Clairvaux.
    - "In the name of tolerance, we are being intolerant." – Charlton Heston.

4. **Surprising Data on Free Speech Restrictions:**
    - **Cato Institute Study:** Found that 58% of Americans believe the political climate prevents them from saying things they believe because others might find them offensive.
    - **Foundation for Individual Rights in Education (FIRE):** Reported that over 90% of colleges have policies that restrict free speech to some extent.

5. **Fun Facts About Debates on College Campuses:**
    - **Free Speech Zones:** Some colleges have designated areas where free speech is allowed, often relegating protests and

public speaking to small, less trafficked areas.

- **Trigger Warnings**: Increasingly used in syllabi to alert students about potentially distressing material, sparking debates about academic freedom and resilience.

6. **Key Legislative Bills Related to Free Speech and Tolerance**:
    - **First Amendment to the U.S. Constitution**: The cornerstone of American free speech, often tested by tolerance policies.
    - **Title IX (Education Amendments of 1972)**: Originally aimed at preventing sex-based discrimination, its interpretation has expanded to include speech codes and harassment policies that sometimes restrict free speech.

7. **Dates and Outcomes of Major Free Speech Controversies**:
    - **2017**: Milo Yiannopoulos' speech at UC Berkeley was canceled due to violent protests, highlighting the clash between free speech and campus safety.
    - **2015**: The University of Missouri protests led to the resignation of the university president over racial issues, sparking a national debate on free speech and race relations.

8. **Notable Politicians Involved in Debates on Tolerance and Free Speech**:
    - **Lyndon B. Johnson**: Instrumental in passing the Civil Rights Act of 1964, which has been central to many debates about free speech and discrimination.
    - **Barack Obama**: Spoke frequently about the importance of free speech and the dangers of "cancel culture," particularly in academic settings.

9. **Comparisons of Tolerance Policies Between Different Institutions**:
    - **Harvard University**: Known for its stringent speech codes and high-profile disinvitation of controversial speakers.
    - **University of Chicago**: Notable for its strong stance on free speech, issuing the "Chicago Principles" to affirm its

commitment to open discourse.

10. **Case Studies of Specific Incidents of Intolerance in the Name of Tolerance:**
    - **Bret Weinstein at Evergreen State College (2017):** A biology professor faced intense backlash and was ultimately forced to resign after he opposed a campus event that asked white students to leave campus for a day.
    - **Nicholas and Erika Christakis at Yale University (2015):** Faced severe backlash and protests after questioning the university's stance on culturally sensitive Halloween costumes, leading to a national discussion on free speech and academic freedom.

11 - The Misguided Notions of Racial Divides

To understand the voting patterns among racial groups, we need to dive into the historical context. The Civil Rights Movement in the 1960s marked a significant shift in American politics, reshaping the political landscape and influencing voting behaviors. Before this period, African Americans were predominantly Republican, influenced by the party of Lincoln, which abolished slavery. However, the Democratic Party's adoption of civil rights legislation under leaders like Lyndon B. Johnson led to a dramatic realignment.

One of the most persistent misconceptions is that racial groups vote monolithically based on party loyalty alone. For instance, the African American community's strong support for the Democratic Party is often seen as a simple loyalty to the party that passed the Civil Rights Act of 1964 and the Voting Rights Act of 1965. However, this support also stems from the Democratic Party's stance on social issues and economic policies that many African Americans feel address their communities' needs better.

The Voting Rights Act of 1965 was a watershed moment, aimed at overcoming legal barriers at the state and local levels that prevented African Americans from exercising their right to vote. This act significantly increased voter turnout among African Americans, particularly in the Southern states, where disenfranchisement had been most pervasive. The Civil Rights Movement and subsequent political shifts further entrenched the Democratic Party's support among African Americans.

underperforming in various socioeconomic measures compared to their counterparts in Red states. Let's dive into the numbers and the reasons behind this paradox.

Take, for example, cities like Chicago, Los Angeles, and Detroit—urban areas that have been under Democratic control for decades. These cities consistently show higher unemployment rates among minorities compared to national averages. According to the Bureau of Labor Statistics, the unemployment rate for African Americans in Chicago was significantly higher than the national average, hovering around 10% compared to the national rate of about 6%. This disparity is often attributed to stringent business regulations and high taxes that discourage investment and job creation.

Crime rates in blue-controlled cities are another critical issue. Cities like Baltimore, St. Louis, and Detroit often top the list for violent crime rates in the United States. The FBI's Uniform Crime Reporting (UCR) Program consistently shows that these cities have some of the highest per capita rates of violent crimes, including homicides and aggravated assaults. Critics argue that progressive criminal justice reforms, such as reduced sentencing and bail reform, although well-intentioned, often lead to a revolving door justice system where repeat offenders are quickly back on the streets.

Homelessness is another area where blue cities and states struggle. California, with its liberal policies, has the highest homeless population in the nation. Cities like San Francisco and Los Angeles have witnessed a homelessness crisis that seems to grow annually. Despite massive spending on homelessness programs—Los Angeles County alone spends over $1 billion annually—the numbers continue to rise. The U.S. Department of Housing and Urban Development's (HUD) 2023 Annual Homeless Assessment Report shows that California accounted for more than half of all unsheltered homeless people in the country.

Economic equality, or the lack thereof, is stark in many blue states. Income inequality in states like New York and California is among the highest in the nation. While these states boast significant economic output and wealth, this wealth is often concentrated among a small percentage of the population. The Gini coefficient, a measure of income inequality, is particularly high in these states. Policies aimed at wealth redistribution, such as high taxes on the wealthy and extensive welfare programs, have not effectively closed the gap. Instead, they sometimes exacerbate the problem by driving businesses and affluent individuals to more tax-friendly environments.

Public education in many blue cities is in a state of crisis. Despite high per-pupil spending, educational outcomes in cities like Detroit, Baltimore, and Philadelphia are dismal. The National Center for Education Statistics (NCES) reports that proficiency rates in reading and math for students in these cities are far below the national average. Issues such as teacher union influence, lack of accountability, and bureaucratic inefficiencies are often cited as reasons for poor performance. For instance, the high school graduation rate in Detroit is just over 70%, compared to the national average of 85%.

It's clear that the realities in many blue-controlled cities and states starkly contrast the promises of their progressive policies. While the intentions behind these policies may be noble, their execution often leaves much to be desired. Higher unemployment, crime, homelessness, economic inequality, and lower quality of education are significant issues that require reevaluation of the current strategies.

Take it from your favorite genius (me)—it's essential to look beyond the surface and understand the multifaceted impacts of political policies. Just because something sounds good in a speech doesn't mean it translates well into practice. Sometimes, the road to a better future requires a hard look at the facts, not just the feelings.

Why Certain Classes Voting Democrat is a Mistake

Certain racial and economic classes have traditionally aligned with the Democratic Party, often believing that its policies will best address their needs and improve their living conditions. However, this loyalty may be misguided. Voting for the same party out of habit rather than careful consideration of actual outcomes can lead to disappointing results.

Democratic policies have sometimes failed to deliver the promised benefits to these groups. Let's break it down:

Economic Impact of Welfare Policies

Welfare policies, intended to provide a safety net, can sometimes create a cycle of dependency rather than fostering economic independence. It's like giving someone a fish every day instead of teaching them to fish—eventually, they start to expect the fish delivery at 5 PM sharp.

The Clinton Era Welfare Reforms: Mixed Results

Take the welfare reforms under President Bill Clinton in the 1990s. The Personal Responsibility and Work Opportunity Reconciliation Act (PRWORA) was meant to be a game-changer, designed to reduce dependency on government assistance and encourage work. The act imposed work requirements and time limits on welfare recipients, theoretically nudging people towards gainful employment. And let's be honest, the name itself—Personal Responsibility and Work Opportunity Reconciliation Act—sounds like it was crafted by a team of PR experts who thought it could inspire even the most committed couch potato to get a job.

Reduced Welfare Rolls: A Double-Edged Sword

Sure, the reforms reduced welfare rolls. Politicians celebrated with high-fives, convinced they'd cracked the code to eliminating poverty. But here's the kicker: while some people did find jobs, many others were left without adequate support, especially during economic downturns. Imagine being told you have to work to earn your keep, but the only available job is juggling flaming swords while riding a unicycle on a tightrope. That's the kind of "opportunity" many faced—great in theory, disastrous in practice.

Dependency vs. Independence: The Eternal Struggle

The goal was to foster economic independence. Instead, for many, it turned into a bureaucratic nightmare. Work requirements? Sure, but what about those who couldn't find stable employment or those who had to care for young children or elderly parents? The safety net morphed into a tightrope, and many fell off. It's like telling someone, "You can have your parachute back after you jump out of the plane." Effective policy-making should be more nuanced than this high-wire act.

The Cycle of Dependency: Reinforced

Instead of breaking the cycle of dependency, PRWORA sometimes reinforced it. How? By creating a revolving door where people were temporarily off welfare rolls but ended up back on them when they couldn't sustain employment. It's like trying to quit your donut addiction by switching to cupcakes—you're still not on the path to a healthy diet.

Economic Downturns: The Unseen Villain

Economic downturns exacerbated the problem. During recessions, when jobs are scarcer than hen's teeth, people were booted off welfare with nowhere to turn. The supposed "safety net" became a trampoline with holes. And guess what happens when you jump on a trampoline with holes? You crash to the ground, hard.

Educational Outcomes in Democrat-Led Districts

Educational policies in urban areas often led by Democratic administrations have not always yielded positive results. Cities like Detroit and Chicago, with long histories of Democratic leadership, continue to struggle with failing public schools despite high spending. The National Center for Education Statistics (NCES) reports that these cities have some of the lowest test scores and graduation rates in the nation. In Detroit, for instance, the public school system's graduation rate is just over 70%, far below the national average. Despite significant investments, the quality of education remains poor, leaving many students ill-prepared for the workforce.

Data and Studies

- **U.S. Census Bureau:** Data shows that poverty rates among African Americans and Hispanics remain high despite decades of Democratic welfare policies. In 2020, the poverty rate for African Americans was 19.5%, and for Hispanics, it was 17%, compared to the national average of 10.5%.
- **Bureau of Labor Statistics:** Unemployment rates among African Americans and Hispanics are consistently higher than the national

average. As of 2021, the unemployment rate for African Americans was 8.2%, while the national rate was 5.4%.

- **Policy Studies:** Research from think tanks such as the Brookings Institution has shown that while welfare programs provide short-term relief, they often fail to address the root causes of poverty, such as lack of access to quality education and job opportunities.

Specific Examples

1. **Welfare Reform Under President Clinton:** The PRWORA of 1996 aimed to end "welfare as we know it." While it succeeded in reducing welfare dependency, it also pushed many families into deeper poverty when they could not meet the work requirements.
2. **Educational Policies in Detroit:** Despite substantial funding, Detroit Public Schools are plagued by low academic performance and high dropout rates. The district's struggles highlight the inefficacy of simply increasing spending without comprehensive reform.
3. **Chicago's Public Education System:** Similar to Detroit, Chicago has faced chronic issues in its public schools, including underperformance, high teacher absenteeism, and inadequate facilities. These problems persist despite the city's Democratic leadership and substantial budget allocations.

Imagine you always order the same meal at your favorite restaurant, even though it makes you sick every time. You keep thinking, "This time it'll be different." But spoiler alert: it's not. Voting Democrat, for some, has become just like that—an unfortunate culinary habit. You hope for a different result, but you end up with the same stomach-ache.

It's abundantly clear that Democratic policies may appear to align with the interests of certain racial and economic classes, the actual outcomes often fall short of the promises. By critically evaluating the impacts of these policies, voters can make more informed decisions rather than relying on habitual loyalty. Take it from genius narrator, sometimes it takes a fresh perspective to see the bigger picture.

Undeniable Facts

1. **Historical Reasons for Racial and Economic Class Alignments with the Democratic Party**
   - **The New Deal (1930s):** Franklin D. Roosevelt's policies aimed at economic recovery during the Great Depression garnered substantial support from lower-income and minority groups.
   - **Civil Rights Movement (1960s):** The Democratic Party's support for civil rights legislation under Presidents Kennedy and Johnson helped align African American voters with the

party.

- **Great Society Programs (1960s):** Lyndon B. Johnson's initiatives to eliminate poverty and racial injustice further solidified the Democratic Party's appeal to economically disadvantaged groups.

2. **Notable Failures of Democrat Policies for Certain Classes**

- **Welfare Reform (1996):** The Personal Responsibility and Work Opportunity Reconciliation Act (PRWORA) reduced welfare dependency but also left many families without adequate support.
- **Public Education in Urban Areas:** Despite high spending, cities like Detroit and Chicago continue to struggle with failing public schools and low academic performance.
- **Affordable Housing Initiatives:** Programs aimed at increasing affordable housing in cities like San Francisco have often led to increased homelessness and housing shortages.

3. **Quotes About the Consequences of Political Alignment**

- **Thomas Sowell:** "The most basic question is not what is best, but who shall decide what is best."
- **Frederick Douglass:** "The Republican party is the ship, all else is the sea."
- **Malcolm X:** "The white liberal is the worst enemy to America, and the worst enemy to the black man."

4. **Surprising Data on Economic and Educational Outcomes**

- **Bureau of Labor Statistics (2021):** Unemployment rates among African Americans and Hispanics are consistently higher than the national average, with African American unemployment at 8.2% compared to the national rate of 5.4%.
- **U.S. Census Bureau:** Despite decades of welfare policies, the poverty rate for African Americans was 19.5% in 2020, significantly higher than the national average of 10.5%.

- **NCES:** Cities with Democratic leadership, like Detroit and Baltimore, have some of the lowest high school graduation rates in the country, often below 70%.

5. **Fun Facts About Political Party Affiliations**
    - **First Black Congresswoman:** Shirley Chisholm, elected in 1968, was a Democrat and a trailblazer for minority representation in Congress.
    - **Naturalized Citizen Impact:** The growing number of naturalized citizens from Asia and Latin America has increasingly influenced U.S. elections, with higher voter turnout rates among these groups.
    - **Shift in Hispanic Voting:** Recent elections have shown a notable increase in Hispanic support for Republican candidates, challenging the assumption of monolithic support for Democrats.

6. **Key Legislative Bills Related to Welfare and Education**
    - **The Personal Responsibility and Work Opportunity Reconciliation Act (1996):** Aimed to reduce welfare dependency through work requirements and time limits.
    - **No Child Left Behind Act (2001):** Intended to improve educational outcomes through standardized testing and accountability measures.
    - **Every Student Succeeds Act (2015):** Replaced No Child Left Behind, giving states more flexibility in education policy while maintaining accountability standards.

7. **Dates and Outcomes of Major Policy Changes**
    - **1965 Voting Rights Act:** Dramatically increased voter registration and turnout among African Americans in the South.
    - **1996 Welfare Reform:** Reduced welfare rolls but also left many families without adequate support, particularly during economic downturns.
    - **2010 Affordable Care Act:** Expanded healthcare coverage

but faced criticism for rising premiums and limited provider networks.

8. **Notable Politicians Known for Their Influence on Class-Based Voting Patterns**
    - **Lyndon B. Johnson:** His Great Society programs aimed at eliminating poverty and racial injustice, influencing minority support for the Democratic Party.
    - **Barack Obama:** His presidency mobilized unprecedented African American voter turnout and reinforced the Democratic Party's appeal to minority groups.
    - **Stacey Abrams:** Known for her efforts to combat voter suppression and increase voter registration and turnout in Georgia.

9. **Comparisons of Policy Impacts Between Democrat and Republican Districts**
    - **Economic Performance:** Republican-led states like Texas and Florida often boast lower taxes and higher job growth compared to Democratic-led states like California and New York.
    - **Education Outcomes:** Studies show that states with more school choice options, often championed by Republicans, tend to have higher student performance and satisfaction.
    - **Crime Rates:** Cities with Democratic leadership, such as Chicago and Baltimore, often report higher crime rates compared to Republican-led cities of similar size.

10. **Case Studies of Specific Communities Affected by Democrat Policies**

- **Detroit, Michigan:** Despite significant federal and state investment, Detroit continues to struggle with high unemployment, crime, and failing public schools.
- **San Francisco, California:** Efforts to increase affordable housing have often backfired, leading to higher homelessness rates and housing shortages.

- **Baltimore, Maryland:** Persistent issues with crime and education highlight the challenges faced by long-term Democratic governance in addressing urban poverty and social inequities.

155

12 - The Rise and Fall of Woke Ideology

Origins and Spread of Woke Culture

Woke culture, like the latest fashion craze, has taken the world by storm. Its roots can be traced back to social justice movements, which have historically aimed to address inequalities and injustices in society. Picture the early 20th century with activists pushing for civil rights, gender equality, and workers' rights. Fast forward to today, and you'll see how these foundational movements evolved, spreading through various sectors of society like wildfire.

Historical Roots of Woke Culture: The term "woke" originally signified awareness of social and racial injustices. The Civil Rights Movement of the 1960s, which fought against racial segregation and discrimination, was a significant precursor. Leaders like Martin Luther King Jr. and Malcolm X championed the cause of equality, laying the groundwork for modern woke culture. These movements emphasized the importance of being "woke" to the systemic injustices that pervade society.

The Spread Through Institutions: Woke ideology has permeated numerous institutions, notably academia, media, and corporate America. In universities, critical race theory and intersectionality have become part of the curriculum, urging students to scrutinize the power structures that perpetuate inequality. Media outlets have adopted woke language and perspectives, often shaping public opinion by highlighting stories that align with social justice narratives. Corporations, not wanting to be left behind, have integrated diversity, equity, and inclusion (DEI) initiatives into their policies. This shift can be seen in hiring practices, marketing campaigns, and corporate social responsibility programs.

The influence of woke culture is evident in various movements and initiatives:

1. **Black Lives Matter (BLM):** The rise of BLM exemplifies the modern iteration of social justice activism. BLM has brought issues of police brutality and racial inequality to the forefront of public consciousness, leveraging social media to mobilize support and effect change. High-profile protests and campaigns have led to significant

discussions and policy proposals aimed at addressing systemic racism.

2. **#MeToo Movement:** This movement has highlighted issues of sexual harassment and assault, particularly in the workplace. By encouraging survivors to share their stories, #MeToo has exposed high-profile offenders and prompted changes in corporate policies and practices regarding sexual harassment and gender equality. It has fostered a cultural shift towards greater accountability and support for victims.

3. **Environmental Justice Initiatives:** Groups like Extinction Rebellion and the Sunrise Movement have combined environmental advocacy with social justice principles, addressing how climate change disproportionately affects marginalized communities. Their efforts have led to increased awareness and action on environmental policies, pushing for systemic changes that consider both ecological sustainability and social equity.

Imagine woke culture as the newest must-have fashion accessory. Everyone's scrambling to get it, even if it doesn't quite fit their style. Suddenly, every institution is strutting around in woke attire, from universities flaunting their critical race theory scarves to corporations donning DEI hats. It's like watching a toddler try on their parent's oversized shoes—utterly ill-fitting and hilariously misguided.

First, you've got academia, proudly displaying its critical race theory scarves as if they're the key to eternal intellectual enlightenment. Professors are now more focused on ensuring everyone knows the correct pronouns than actually teaching useful skills. It's a real hoot to watch students graduate with a degree in Woke Studies, only to realize their job prospects are as bleak as a rain-soaked parade.

Then there are the corporations, each one tripping over the other to showcase their DEI hats. These companies are so desperate to prove they're "woke" that they'll hire a Diversity Officer before they even hire a CEO. You've got executives patting themselves on the back for their progressive policies while they outsource labor to countries with atrocious human rights records. But hey, as long as their social media profiles are covered in rainbow flags and BLM hashtags, they're golden, right?

Government agencies aren't far behind, of course. They've jumped on the woke bandwagon too, enacting policies that make a DMV visit feel like a seminar on intersectionality. You'll need to check your privilege at the door and complete a micro-aggression sensitivity training before you can renew your driver's license. It's all about keeping up appearances, even if it means creating more red tape than a bureaucratic nightmare.

Even the entertainment industry is getting in on the act. Hollywood's latest trend is to remake classic movies with diverse casts, not because it enhances the story, but because it's the woke thing to do. Forget about originality or artistic integrity—what matters is ticking those diversity boxes. Who cares if the movie tanks at the box office? At least they can claim moral superiority while counting their losses.

Finally, social media platforms are the true catwalks of woke culture. Influencers and celebrities compete to out-woke each other, posting performative activism at every opportunity. They'll preach about saving the planet from their private jets and lecture about wealth inequality from their mansions. It's a spectacle that makes you wonder if they even believe the nonsense they're spouting or if it's all just for likes and retweets.

It's a sight to behold—like watching everyone at a party awkwardly dance to a song they just heard for the first time. They're all out of sync, stepping on each other's toes, but convinced they're part of the coolest trend ever. The absurdity is almost poetic.

Data and Studies: Several studies have documented the spread and impact of woke ideology. For example, research published in academic journals highlights how critical race theory has influenced educational curricula and pedagogy. Media analysis reports illustrate the shift in narrative framing and language in news outlets. Social science research provides insights into the effects of DEI initiatives in the workplace, showing both positive outcomes and areas needing improvement.

Specific Examples:

- **Black Lives Matter:** The BLM movement gained global attention after the deaths of individuals like George Floyd and Breonna Taylor. Its use of social media activism has been particularly effective in raising awareness and prompting discussions about racial justice.

- **DEI Initiatives in Corporations:** Companies like Google and Microsoft have implemented comprehensive DEI programs, aiming to increase the diversity of their workforce and create a more inclusive corporate culture. These initiatives often include training programs, mentorship opportunities, and policies designed to eliminate bias in hiring and promotion.

Sad really, but let's face it. Woke culture, with its roots in historical social justice movements, has rapidly spread through academia, media, and corporate America, influencing a wide range of societal aspects. Whether it's through critical race theory, intersectionality, or DEI initiatives, the impact of woke ideology is unmistakable, even if, like the latest fashion trend, it sometimes feels like everyone's trying to keep up with the latest style, whether it suits them or not.

Undeniable Facts

Key Moments in the History of Social Justice Movements:

- **The Civil Rights Movement (1950s-1960s):** This period was pivotal in fighting racial segregation and discrimination in the United States, leading to significant legislation like the Civil Rights Act of 1964.
- **The Stonewall Riots (1969):** Sparked the modern LGBTQ+ rights movement, leading to the establishment of annual Pride parades.
- **#MeToo Movement (2017):** Brought global attention to sexual harassment and assault, leading to widespread changes in workplace policies and awareness.

1. **Notable Figures in the Rise of Woke Culture:**
   - **Kimberlé Crenshaw:** Coined the term "intersectionality," highlighting how various forms of discrimination overlap.
   - **Ta-Nehisi Coates:** Author and journalist known for his work on systemic racism and white supremacy.
   - **Greta Thunberg:** Young climate activist who emphasizes the intersection of environmental justice and social equity.

2. **Quotes About the Spread of Woke Ideology:**
   - "Stay woke." – Erykah Badu, popularizing the term in the context of social awareness.
   - "There is no such thing as a single-issue struggle because we do not live single-issue lives." – Audre Lorde, emphasizing the interconnectedness of various social justice issues.
   - "Injustice anywhere is a threat to justice everywhere." – Martin Luther King Jr., encapsulating the ethos of social justice movements.

3. **Surprising Statistics on the Adoption of Woke Practices in Institutions:**
   - Over 75% of Fortune 500 companies have implemented DEI (Diversity, Equity, and Inclusion) programs as of 2022.
   - A 2020 survey found that 60% of U.S. colleges and universities had incorporated critical race theory into their curricula.
   - Public school districts in 36 states have adopted policies based on social-emotional learning (SEL), which includes elements of woke ideology.

4. **Fun Facts About Early Social Justice Activism:**
   - The first organized women's rights convention, held in Seneca Falls in 1848, marked the beginning of the women's suffrage movement in the United States.
   - Labor unions in the early 20th century were among the first to advocate for workers' rights and fair labor practices, laying the groundwork for modern social justice efforts.

5. **Key Legislative Bills Related to Social Justice and DEI Initiatives:**

- **Civil Rights Act of 1964:** Prohibited discrimination on the basis of race, color, religion, sex, or national origin.
- **Americans with Disabilities Act of 1990:** Ensured rights and protections for individuals with disabilities.
- **Title IX (1972):** Prohibited sex-based discrimination in federally funded education programs.

6. **Dates and Outcomes of Major Social Justice Campaigns:**
   - **Selma to Montgomery Marches (1965):** Led to the passage of the Voting Rights Act of 1965.
   - **March on Washington for Jobs and Freedom (1963):** Culminated in MLK's "I Have a Dream" speech and bolstered the push for civil rights legislation.
   - **Women's March (2017):** A global protest advocating for women's rights, equality, and other social justice issues.

7. **Notable Academics and Activists Known for Promoting Woke Ideology:**
   - **Angela Davis:** Activist and scholar known for her work on prison reform and racial justice.
   - **Ibram X. Kendi:** Author of "How to Be an Antiracist," which has influenced discussions on systemic racism.
   - **Judith Butler:** Philosopher and gender theorist whose work on gender performativity has shaped modern gender studies.

8. **Comparisons of Woke Culture Adoption in Different Sectors:**
   - **Education:** Higher education institutions have rapidly adopted woke culture, integrating it into curricula and campus policies.
   - **Corporate:** Companies have embraced DEI initiatives, often tied to brand image and corporate responsibility.
   - **Entertainment:** Hollywood has increasingly focused on diversity in casting and storytelling, reflecting woke cultural values.

9. **Case Studies of Specific Institutions and Their Transformation Due to Woke Culture:**

- ○ **Starbucks:** Implemented extensive racial bias training for employees following a high-profile incident in 2018.
- ○ **Google:** Established various DEI programs and faced both praise and criticism for its handling of diversity issues within the company.
- ○ **University of California:** Integrated critical race theory into multiple disciplines, sparking debates on academic freedom and educational priorities.

Factual Reasons Why Woke Ideology is a Losing Concept

Woke ideology, despite its surge in popularity, has significant flaws that often lead to negative outcomes. Much like a trendy diet fad that promises miracles but leaves you starving and disillusioned, woke ideology tends to overpromise and underdeliver, causing more harm than good in the long run.

Practical and Philosophical Issues with Woke Ideology: At its core, woke ideology seeks to address social injustices and promote equality. However, its approach often leads to philosophical inconsistencies and practical challenges. The emphasis on identity politics, for example, can create a fragmented society where individuals are viewed primarily through the lens of their race, gender, or sexual orientation, rather than as unique individuals. This focus on group identity can undermine social cohesion and foster division.

Division, Censorship, and Inefficiency: Woke policies frequently lead to division, censorship, and inefficiency. The insistence on safe spaces and trigger warnings on college campuses, while intended to protect students, often results in the stifling of free speech and open debate. Universities, once bastions of free thought, are now riddled with censorship, where controversial ideas are suppressed rather than discussed. According to the Foundation for Individual Rights in Education (FIRE), over 60% of colleges have policies that substantially restrict free speech.

Backlash Against Cancel Culture: Cancel culture, a prominent feature of woke ideology, aims to hold individuals accountable for offensive or problematic behavior. However, it often devolves into public shaming and ostracism for minor infractions or old mistakes. This has led to a societal atmosphere where people are afraid to speak openly or engage in meaningful dialogue. A Pew Research Center study found that 44% of Americans have felt pressure to censor themselves due to fear of backlash from cancel culture.

Stifling Free Speech on College Campuses: The rise of safe spaces and trigger warnings on college campuses has significantly impacted the landscape of free speech. While these measures aim to create inclusive environments, they often result in the exclusion of dissenting viewpoints. For instance, high-profile disinvitations of speakers and protests against controversial figures have become commonplace. A 2019 survey by the Knight Foundation revealed that 68% of college students believe that the climate on their campus prevents people from saying things they believe, because others might find them offensive.

Inefficacy of Performative Activism: Performative activism, where actions are taken more for public recognition than actual impact, is another issue with woke ideology. Corporations and individuals often engage in symbolic gestures—like changing social media profiles or releasing statements—without implementing meaningful changes. This superficial approach does little to address the underlying issues and can actually detract from genuine efforts for social justice. For example, many companies that publicly support social causes continue to engage in practices that contradict their stated values, undermining their credibility and the broader movement.

Controversies Surrounding "Safe Spaces": The concept of safe spaces, designed to protect marginalized groups from harm, has sparked significant debate. Critics argue that these spaces, while well-intentioned, create echo chambers where individuals are shielded from opposing viewpoints. This can hinder intellectual growth and resilience. A 2018 study by the Heterodox Academy found that students exposed to a diversity of perspectives are better equipped to handle controversial issues and develop critical thinking skills.

Economic Impacts of Boycotts Driven by Woke Activism: Boycotts driven by woke activism can have unintended economic consequences. While these boycotts aim to hold companies accountable, they often lead to job losses and economic instability, particularly affecting low-wage workers. For instance, the boycott against Goya Foods in 2020, initiated due to the CEO's political statements, sparked significant controversy and had mixed economic impacts. While some consumers supported the boycott, others rallied to support the company, highlighting the divisive nature of such actions.

Woke Ideology as a Fad Diet

Think of woke ideology as the latest diet fad that promises to cleanse you from all societal toxins and transform you into a paragon of virtue and enlightenment. It's like that magic detox tea that guarantees to make you lose 20 pounds in a week but actually just leaves you dehydrated and miserable.

Woke culture is the kale smoothie of political ideologies—everyone swears by it, but deep down, no one really enjoys choking it down. Institutions are desperately gulping it up, hoping it will magically fix everything, from racial inequality to workplace diversity. But much like that overpriced green juice, it's all show and no substance, leaving everyone involved hungry for real solutions and slightly nauseated from the virtue-signaling overload.

Universities are the worst offenders, eagerly adopting woke policies like they're the secret to academic immortality. They've become sanctuaries of hypersensitivity where students are coddled with safe spaces and trigger warnings, turning campuses into daycare centers for adults. Imagine trying to learn how to navigate the complexities of the real world when you're constantly shielded from even the mildest discomforts. It's like signing up for a boot camp where the toughest challenge is a guided meditation session.

Then there's the corporate world, where CEOs don their DEI hats with all the sincerity of a used car salesman. They roll out performative initiatives faster than you can say "virtue signaling," all while continuing their dubious business practices behind the scenes. It's the equivalent of a fast-food chain launching a "healthy" menu that consists of a single sad salad amidst a sea of grease and sugar. Sure, they talk a big game about inclusivity, but when it comes to actual impact, they're as hollow as a gluten-free donut.

The entertainment industry, of course, jumps on the bandwagon too. Hollywood is remaking classics with diverse casts not because it enhances the story, but because it's the woke thing to do. It's like rebooting an old TV show but replacing every character with a cardboard cutout that checks all the diversity boxes. The plot remains just as thin, and the audience is left wondering why they even bothered.

Social media influencers are perhaps the most insufferable, turning woke culture into a performance art. They preach about saving the planet from their private jets and decry wealth inequality from their palatial estates. Their brand of activism is as genuine as a three-dollar bill, more concerned with likes and retweets than any meaningful change. They're the diet gurus of the ideological world, peddling empty promises that do little more than inflate their egos and bank accounts.

So, if you're thinking about hopping on the woke bandwagon, remember this: it's like starting a diet that promises to make you healthier and happier, but in reality, it leaves you weak, confused, and craving something real. Woke ideology is the snake oil of modern culture—slick, seductive, and ultimately, utterly ineffective.

Undeniable Facts

1. **Historical Critiques of Similar Ideological Movements:**
    ◦ **McCarthyism (1950s):** Like woke culture, McCarthyism

led to widespread fear, censorship, and social ostracism. Critics highlighted its paranoia and destruction of careers over unproven allegations.

- **The Cultural Revolution (1966-1976):** Mao's campaign in China aimed to preserve communist ideology, resulting in widespread persecution and the suppression of dissent.
- **Prohibition (1920-1933):** Intended to curb alcohol consumption, it instead led to organized crime and was widely viewed as a moral crusade that failed spectacularly.

2. **Notable Failures of Woke Policies and Initiatives:**

- **Seattle's CHOP Zone (2020):** An autonomous zone created to eliminate police presence devolved into chaos, with increased crime and violence.
- **San Francisco's Public Restroom Initiative:** Aimed at addressing homelessness, it faced criticism for mismanagement and lack of effectiveness, with some restrooms costing over $1 million each without resolving the underlying issues.
- **Evergreen State College (2017):** Policies encouraging racial segregation for sensitivity training led to protests and chaos on campus, significantly impacting enrollment and reputation.

3. **Quotes from Critics of Woke Ideology:**

- "Woke culture is divisive, exclusionary, and hateful. It basically gives mean people a shield to be mean and cruel, armored in false virtue." – Elon Musk
- "The woke mob wants to take your job, your livelihood, your career, your business, and your soul. They want to destroy you." – Ben Shapiro
- "Political correctness is tyranny with manners." – Charlton Heston

4. **Surprising Data on the Impacts of Woke Policies:**

- A 2021 study by the National Association of Scholars found that 74% of college students self-censor in the classroom,

fearing repercussions for expressing non-woke viewpoints.
- According to the Cato Institute, 62% of Americans say they have political views they're afraid to share, with fear of societal backlash being a significant factor.
- An analysis by the Manhattan Institute revealed that DEI training programs often have little to no impact on reducing workplace discrimination and can sometimes exacerbate tensions.

5. **Fun Facts About Ideological Debates in History:**
   - The Federalist vs. Anti-Federalist debates shaped the U.S. Constitution, with fierce arguments over the balance of power between state and federal governments.
   - The Scopes Monkey Trial (1925) highlighted the conflict between science and religion, with intense public and media interest in the debate over evolution.
   - The debates between Thomas Jefferson and Alexander Hamilton in the 1790s set the stage for the U.S. two-party system, with foundational ideological clashes over the role of government.

6. **Key Legislative Responses to Woke-Driven Policies:**
   - **Executive Order on Combating Race and Sex Stereotyping (2020):** Issued by President Trump to prohibit federal funding for training that promotes divisive concepts.
   - **The Stop WOKE Act (2022):** Passed in Florida, aiming to regulate how race and gender issues are taught in schools and discussed in workplaces.
   - **Title VI of the Civil Rights Act (1964):** Initially focused on ending segregation, its modern application sometimes intersects with woke-driven diversity policies, leading to legal battles over its interpretation.

7. **Dates and Outcomes of Significant Woke-Related Controversies:**
   - **James Damore's Google Memo (2017):** Damore was fired after criticizing Google's diversity practices, sparking a global

debate on corporate culture and freedom of speech.

- **Gillette's "The Best Men Can Be" Ad (2019):** The commercial addressing toxic masculinity received both praise and backlash, impacting the brand's market performance.
- **Harvard's Asian-American Admissions Lawsuit (2014-2020):** The lawsuit alleged discrimination against Asian-American applicants in the name of diversity, leading to a Supreme Court case on affirmative action.

8. **Notable Public Figures Who Have Spoken Against Woke Culture:**
   - **Jordan Peterson:** A clinical psychologist who criticizes political correctness and compelled speech.
   - **J.K. Rowling:** Faced backlash for her views on gender identity, sparking widespread debate on free speech and cancel culture.
   - **Joe Rogan:** Host of a popular podcast, he frequently discusses the negative impacts of woke culture on free discourse.

9. **Comparisons of Public Opinion on Woke Ideology Across Different Demographics:**
   - **Younger vs. Older Generations:** Pew Research Center found that younger people are more likely to support woke ideas, while older generations are generally more skeptical.
   - **Political Affiliations:** A Gallup poll showed that liberals are more supportive of woke culture, while conservatives and moderates are increasingly critical.
   - **Geographic Differences:** Urban areas tend to be more supportive of woke policies compared to rural regions, reflecting broader cultural divides.

10. **Case Studies of Communities or Organizations Negatively Impacted by Woke Policies:**
    - **Smith College (2020):** A false racial profiling accusation

led to staff firings and a climate of fear and mistrust on campus.

- **The ACLU's Free Speech Crisis:** The organization faced internal conflict over its support for free speech versus woke-driven advocacy, leading to a shift in its traditional mission.
- **Portland, Oregon:** Prolonged protests and woke-driven policy changes have led to increased crime rates and economic decline in certain areas, prompting a reevaluation of local governance strategies.

13 - Immigration and the Rule of Law

The Liberal Drive for Open Borders

Liberal policies often champion the idea of open borders and more lenient immigration laws, imagining a utopian world where everyone gets along just fine. But let's dive into why this idealistic vision can lead to some very real challenges.

The Liberal Push for Open Borders: Liberals frequently advocate for policies that make it easier for immigrants to enter and stay in the country. These policies range from supporting the Deferred Action for Childhood Arrivals (DACA) program to promoting the idea of sanctuary cities that shield undocumented immigrants from federal law enforcement. The underlying belief is that open borders and lenient immigration laws are humane and just, providing opportunities for those seeking a better life.

Challenges and Consequences: However, this idealistic approach often overlooks the practical consequences. Imagine leaving your front door wide open and then being shocked when your living room is packed with strangers. Open border policies can lead to increased illegal immigration, putting a strain on public resources like healthcare, education, and social services. For instance, sanctuary cities such as San Francisco and Los Angeles, while well-intentioned, often face significant challenges in managing the influx of undocumented immigrants.

Examples and Legislative Efforts:

- **Sanctuary Cities:** Cities like San Francisco have adopted policies that limit cooperation with federal immigration authorities, intending to protect undocumented immigrants. While these cities aim to create safe havens, they also encounter issues such as higher crime rates and overburdened public services. The impact on local resources can be significant, with taxpayers often footing the bill.
- **DACA Program:** The DACA program, implemented during the Obama administration, allows undocumented individuals brought to the U.S. as children to stay and work legally. While it provides much-needed relief to these individuals, it has also sparked heated debates

over its long-term implications and the message it sends about illegal immigration.

- **The DREAM Act:** Proposed multiple times in Congress, the DREAM Act aims to provide a pathway to citizenship for undocumented immigrants brought to the U.S. as children. Though it garners significant support, critics argue it encourages more illegal immigration by offering incentives without addressing border security.

- **California's Sanctuary Laws:** California has some of the most lenient immigration policies in the nation, with laws that limit state and local law enforcement from cooperating with federal immigration authorities. These laws have led to contentious debates about state versus federal authority and the effectiveness of such policies in maintaining public safety and order.

Data and Studies:

According to the Department of Homeland Security (DHS), illegal border crossings have surged significantly in 2024. The U.S. Customs and Border Protection (CBP) reported over 8 million encounters at the southwest border since President Biden took office. This figure highlights the unprecedented levels of migration and the ongoing challenges in managing border security.

Let's look at the numbers over the past three administrations to understand the trend:

- Obama Administration (2009-2017): During President Obama's tenure, there were nearly 5.5 million encounters at the U.S.-Mexico border. This period saw significant fluctuations, including a notable peak in 2014 due to the increase in unaccompanied minors from Central America.

- Trump Administration (2017-2021): Under President Trump, the border security strategy focused on stringent immigration policies, including the construction of a border wall and the implementation of the "Remain in Mexico" policy. Despite these measures, CBP recorded approximately 3.3 million encounters during his term. The fiscal year 2019 saw a significant spike, with over 1 million encounters, largely attributed to changes in asylum policies and migrant caravans from Central America.

- Biden Administration (2021-Present): Since President Biden took office, there have been over 9.5 million encounters nationwide, with more than 7.8 million at the southwest border. This dramatic increase is attributed to a combination of factors, including policy reversals, the end of Title 42 expulsions, and continued socio-economic instability in migrants' home countries.

These figures underscore the escalating challenges in managing illegal border crossings and the varying impacts of different administration policies. The surge under the Biden administration has been particularly notable, with monthly encounters frequently setting new records and significantly straining border management resources.Pew Research Center reports that while a substantial portion of Americans support pathways to citizenship for undocumented immigrants, there is also significant concern about the strain on public resources and the need for stronger border controls.

Studies by the Center for Immigration Studies (CIS) highlight the economic impact of illegal immigration, pointing to increased costs in public education, healthcare, and welfare services.

Think of open border policies like leaving your front door wide open and then being surprised when your house gets crowded. You might think you're being hospitable, but soon enough, you're out of snacks, the bathroom line is endless, and someone's taken over your favorite chair. Sure, you meant well, but now your home's a chaotic free-for-all. Similarly, liberal immigration policies might start with good intentions, but the real-world consequences can quickly turn your welcoming space into a crowded, unmanageable mess.

Undeniable Facts

1. **Historical Examples of Open Border Policies:**
    - **Ancient Rome:** The Roman Empire often encouraged migration and resettlement within its borders to boost the economy and secure its frontiers.
    - **Medieval Spain:** During the Reconquista, various Spanish kingdoms encouraged settlement in newly conquered territories to bolster their hold on the land.
2. **Notable Figures and Their Stance on Immigration Reform:**

- **Ronald Reagan:** Supported the Immigration Reform and Control Act of 1986, which granted amnesty to millions of undocumented immigrants.
- **Barack Obama:** Implemented the Deferred Action for Childhood Arrivals (DACA) program, providing temporary protection to undocumented immigrants brought to the U.S. as children.

3. **Quotes About the Challenges of Open Borders:**
   - "A nation without borders is not a nation." – Ronald Reagan
   - "You either have a country or you don't have a country." – Donald Trump

4. **Surprising Statistics on Illegal Immigration:**
   - In 2024, over 8 million encounters were reported at the southwest border since President Biden took office, reflecting a significant increase compared to previous administrations.
   - A Pew Research Center study found that nearly 11 million unauthorized immigrants were living in the U.S. as of 2020.

5. **Fun Facts About Immigration Laws Around the World:**
   - **Canada:** Has a points-based immigration system, where applicants are scored on factors like language proficiency, education, and work experience.
   - **New Zealand:** Offers a visa specifically for wealthy investors who are willing to invest a substantial amount in the country's economy.

6. **Key Legislative Bills Related to Immigration Reform:**
   - **Immigration Reform and Control Act (1986):** Granted amnesty to millions of undocumented immigrants while imposing stricter penalties on employers who hired illegal workers.
   - **DREAM Act:** Proposed multiple times to provide a pathway to citizenship for undocumented immigrants brought to the U.S. as children but has yet to pass Congress.

7. **Dates and Outcomes of Major Immigration Initiatives:**

- ◦ **DACA (2012):** Implemented by President Obama, providing temporary protection to undocumented immigrants brought to the U.S. as children.
  - ◦ **Operation Wetback (1954):** A controversial program aimed at deporting illegal Mexican immigrants, resulting in the removal of over one million individuals.
8. **Notable Politicians Known for Their Immigration Policies:**
   - ◦ **Donald Trump:** Advocated for building a border wall and implemented policies like the "Remain in Mexico" program.
   - ◦ **Kamala Harris:** As Vice President, she has focused on addressing the root causes of migration from Central America. At least, that's the task she was assigned. Still waiting for her to actually do something. Not to worry. It's only been a couple years. I'm sure she'll get to it one of these days.
9. **Comparisons of Immigration Policies Between Liberal and Conservative States:**
   - ◦ **California:** Known for its sanctuary policies, which limit cooperation with federal immigration enforcement.
   - ◦ **Texas:** Implements strict immigration laws and actively cooperates with federal immigration authorities.
10. **Case Studies of Specific Cities or States with Open Border Policies:**
    - ◦ **San Francisco, California:** Known for its sanctuary city status, which has led to both praise for protecting immigrant communities and criticism for allegedly increasing crime.
    - ◦ **Chicago, Illinois:** Another sanctuary city that provides various protections and services to undocumented immigrants, facing similar debates over its impact on local resources and public safety.

Enforcing Laws Selectively and Voter ID Controversies

Let's take a candid look at the chaotic landscape of selective law enforcement and the hypocritical voter ID debates. The Biden administration, with its nearly 100 executive orders undoing previous border policies, has turned the U.S. immigration system into a tragicomedy of errors. Imagine a referee who only calls fouls on one team—welcome to America's selective enforcement circus.

Selective Enforcement of Immigration Laws: Biden's border policies have been a masterclass in neglect and strategic incompetence. With over 8 million illegal border crossings since he took office, the administration's response has been to blame the "broken system" and pass the buck to Congress. Yet, this didn't stop Biden from signing a flurry of executive orders that effectively dismantled Trump-era enforcement measures. The message is clear: laws exist, but they only apply when politically convenient.

Consider sanctuary cities like San Francisco and Los Angeles, where local governments proudly defy federal immigration laws. These cities refuse to cooperate with Immigration and Customs Enforcement (ICE), creating safe havens for illegal immigrants. The result? Overburdened public services and increased crime rates, all while the federal government turns a blind eye. It's like a homeowner opening the door to burglars and then complaining about theft.

In 2023 alone, ICE reported over 1.9 million encounters at the southwest border, a 40% increase compared to previous years. Despite these staggering numbers, enforcement remains inconsistent, leading to a surge in illegal immigration and a strain on resources.

Voter ID Laws Controversies: Now, let's pivot to the voter ID debacle. States like Georgia and Texas have implemented strict voter ID laws, arguing that they prevent fraud and ensure election integrity. Critics, however, decry these measures as discriminatory and burdensome. The Brennan Center for Justice reports that such laws disproportionately affect minorities and low-income voters, who are less likely to possess the required identification.

The irony is palpable. On one hand, the government is lax on immigration enforcement, allowing millions to enter the country illegally. On the other hand, it imposes stringent ID requirements on legal citizens wishing to vote. It's like demanding a passport to enter your own bathroom while leaving the front door wide open for strangers.

Examples of Inconsistent Law Enforcement:

- **Sanctuary Cities:** Cities like Chicago and New York City not only refuse to cooperate with ICE but also provide services like healthcare and legal aid to undocumented immigrants. This defiance creates a patchwork of enforcement where the rule of law is anything but uniform.

How ironic that they complain the most about the sudden surge of illegal immigrants swarming their cities and sucking up all their resources.

- **Voter ID Laws:** The legal battles over these laws are endless. In Texas, for example, the 2011 voter ID law was struck down by federal courts, only to be re-enacted with minor changes in 2017. The result is confusion and frustration among voters who are caught in the crossfire of partisan politics.

Imagine a referee in a basketball game who only calls fouls on one team. Players on the favored team can get away with murder—elbows, trips, you name it—while the other team gets penalized for breathing too hard. This is the absurd reality of selective law enforcement in America. Some laws are strictly enforced, others are ignored, and the rationale often depends on who stands to benefit politically.

Wrapping it all up with duct tape and hoping it holds, the Biden administration's approach to immigration and voter ID laws exemplifies a broader trend of selective enforcement and political grandstanding. It's a hypocritical, irrational cycle where laws are applied inconsistently, leading to societal chaos and eroding trust in the rule of law. Whether it's turning a blind eye to illegal immigration or imposing draconian voter ID requirements, the inconsistency is glaring—and the consequences, disastrous.

<u>SIDE NOTE</u>: Amid all this nonsense, they've managed to approve hundreds and hundreds of billions of dollars to help Ukraine defend their borders. Can you spell D-O-U-B-L-E standard?

Make no mistake. That's not a disparaging comment toward Ukraine, or Israel, or any other countries we help. Nothing wrong with the big kids helping the little kids on the playground. But why aren't we placing just as high a concern on our own situation? Why isn't our own sovereignty as important as that of the smaller countries we support?

Inquiring minds want to know.

Undeniable Facts

1. **Historical Instances of Selective Law Enforcement:**
   - **Prohibition Era (1920-1933):** Selective enforcement of alcohol bans led to widespread corruption and the rise of organized crime. While some regions turned a blind eye, others strictly enforced the laws.
   - **Jim Crow Laws (1877-1965):** These laws enforced racial segregation in the Southern United States, selectively targeting African Americans while allowing white citizens to circumvent legal consequences.

2. **Notable Controversies Over Voter ID Laws:**
   - **Georgia (2021):** The passing of SB 202, which introduced stricter voter ID requirements, sparked national debate and lawsuits alleging voter suppression.
   - **Texas (2011):** Texas implemented a stringent voter ID law that was challenged in court multiple times for allegedly discriminating against minority voters.

3. **Quotes About the Rule of Law and Selective Enforcement:**
   - "Laws are like sausages, it is better not to see them being made." – Otto von Bismarck
   - "There is no greater tyranny than that which is perpetrated under the shield of the law and in the name of justice." – Montesquieu

4. **Surprising Data on Voter Fraud and ID Requirements:**
   - A study by the Brennan Center for Justice found that voter fraud is extremely rare, occurring between 0.0003% and 0.0025% of all votes cast.
   - Pew Research Center data shows that 76% of Americans support requiring photo ID to vote, despite the controversies surrounding its implementation.

5. **Fun Facts About Election Laws in Different Countries:**
   - **Australia:** Voting is compulsory, and citizens are fined for failing to vote without a valid reason.
   - **India:** The world's largest democracy, India uses electronic voting machines (EVMs) in its elections to prevent fraud and improve efficiency.

6. **Key Legislative Bills Related to Voter ID and Immigration Enforcement:**
   - **Voter ID:** The Help America Vote Act (HAVA) of 2002 aimed to improve voting systems and voter access, including identification requirements.
   - **Immigration Enforcement:** The Secure Fence Act of 2006 authorized the construction of physical barriers along the U.S.-Mexico border to enhance border security.

7. **Dates and Outcomes of Major Legal Battles Over These Issues:**
   - **Shelby County v. Holder (2013):** The Supreme Court struck down key provisions of the Voting Rights Act, leading to a surge in new voter ID laws.
   - **Arizona v. United States (2012):** The Supreme Court ruled on the legality of Arizona's controversial immigration law SB 1070, upholding some provisions while striking down others.

8. **Notable Politicians Involved in Voter ID and Immigration Law Debates:**

Stacey Abrams:

Stacey Abrams has been a prominent advocate against strict voter ID laws, arguing that they disproportionately disenfranchise minority and low-income voters. After her narrow defeat in the 2018 Georgia gubernatorial race, Abrams founded Fair Fight Action, an organization focused on voting rights and combating voter suppression. She has been vocal about the barriers that strict ID requirements pose, particularly for marginalized communities who may have difficulty obtaining the necessary documentation. Abrams' advocacy played a significant role in the national dialogue on voting rights, especially leading up to the 2020 presidential election.

Donald Trump:

During his presidency, Donald Trump placed a strong emphasis on voter fraud allegations, despite widespread evidence that such fraud is exceedingly rare. His administration's rhetoric and policies focused on tightening voter ID laws and implementing measures aimed at preventing what he claimed was widespread electoral fraud. Trump's focus on immigration was equally stringent, with policies such as the "Remain in Mexico" program and increased ICE raids. His administration also pushed for the construction of a border wall, aiming to curb illegal immigration and strengthen national security.

Kamala Harris:

As Vice President, Kamala Harris has been a key figure in addressing immigration reform and voting rights. She has advocated for a pathway to citizenship for undocumented immigrants and has been involved in efforts to address the root causes of migration from Central America. On voting rights, Harris has been a vocal critic (between awkward cackles) of restrictive voter ID laws and has supported federal legislation like the For the People Act and the John Lewis Voting Rights Advancement Act, aimed at expanding voter access and preventing discrimination at the polls.

Greg Abbott:

Texas Governor Greg Abbott has been a staunch supporter of strict voter ID laws and aggressive immigration enforcement. Under his leadership, Texas has implemented some of the nation's toughest voter ID requirements, which critics argue suppress minority voting. Abbott has also been a proponent of strong border security measures, including sending the National Guard to the border and supporting the construction of a border wall. His policies reflect a broader conservative approach to both voter ID laws and immigration enforcement.

Comparisons of Law Enforcement Practices Between Liberal and Conservative States:

- **California vs. Texas:** California's sanctuary policies protect undocumented immigrants from federal enforcement, while Texas enforces strict immigration laws and cooperates closely with federal authorities.
- **New York vs. Georgia:** New York has more lenient voter ID requirements compared to Georgia's stringent laws, reflecting broader ideological differences in voting accessibility.

1. **Case Studies of Specific Communities Impacted by Selective Law Enforcement and Voter ID Laws:**
   - **Ferguson, Missouri (2014):** The shooting of Michael Brown and subsequent protests highlighted issues of racial bias and selective law enforcement in predominantly African American communities. The Department of Justice's investigation revealed systematic discrimination and excessive force used by the Ferguson Police Department, contributing to deep mistrust between law enforcement and

the community.

- **North Carolina:** The state's strict voter ID laws, which were struck down in 2016 for targeting African Americans "with almost surgical precision," illustrate the contentious nature of voter ID requirements and their impact on minority voters. The court ruling emphasized that the laws disproportionately affected African Americans, leading to significant debates over voter suppression and electoral fairness.

- **Maricopa County, Arizona:** Under the leadership of former Sheriff Joe Arpaio, Maricopa County became notorious for its aggressive and controversial immigration enforcement tactics. Arpaio's practices, including racial profiling and harsh detention conditions, led to numerous lawsuits and a federal conviction for contempt of court, highlighting severe issues of selective law enforcement and civil rights violations.

- **Texas (SB4 Law, 2017):** Texas Senate Bill 4, also known as the "sanctuary cities ban," required local law enforcement to cooperate with federal immigration authorities. The law faced significant backlash for potentially encouraging racial profiling and undermining trust between immigrant communities and the police. Legal challenges and protests erupted, illustrating the divisive impact of the law on communities across Texas.

- **New York City (Stop-and-Frisk Policy):** The NYPD's stop-and-frisk policy, heavily implemented in the early 2000s, disproportionately targeted Black and Latino individuals. A federal judge ruled in 2013 that the policy violated constitutional rights, leading to widespread criticism of racial profiling and selective law enforcement practices. The policy's impact on community relations and trust in law enforcement remains a critical issue in discussions of policing and civil rights.

14 - Cultural Shifts and Censorship

The term political correctness, which aims to create a society of inclusivity and kindness, often has unintended consequences that result in spectacular failures. Originally designed to protect individuals' emotions and foster a peaceful environment, it has now transformed into the playground bully, relentlessly silencing anyone who dares to deviate from conventional norms.

The PC Police: Stifling Open Dialogue

Imagine a game of "Simon Says" where "Simon" is an overly sensitive hall monitor who takes offense at the slightest hesitation. Go against the norm, and you'll be met with the fury of those who adhere to political correctness. The original intention was noble: to create a society where the sights and sounds of respect fill the air, making everyone feel valued. Yet in reality, it frequently constrains open dialogue and the sharing of diverse perspectives. When you're constantly worried about saying the "wrong" thing, your words lose their meaning and become empty.

Campus Craziness: The Free Speech Fiasco

Let's dive into the battlegrounds of political correctness: college campuses. These supposed bastions of free thought are now the epicenters of speech suppression. Remember when universities were about exploring new ideas and challenging the status quo? Good times.

Today, we're dealing with "safe spaces" and speech codes that could make Orwell blush. Safe spaces were meant to be havens from hate, but they've turned into echo chambers where dissenting opinions are as welcome as a skunk at a garden party. And speech codes? They're the unspoken rules of "Simon Says," but this time, the punishment for missteps is real.

For instance, take the deplatforming of controversial speakers like Ben Shapiro and Jordan Peterson. These guys are hardly the boogeymen of free speech, yet their mere presence on campus triggers protests that resemble a medieval witch hunt. According to the Foundation for Individual Rights in Education (FIRE), over half of U.S. colleges maintain policies that substantially restrict freedom of speech . The American Civil Liberties Union (ACLU) has also raised alarms about this trend, noting that true free speech includes protecting speech we don't like, because one day, that unpopular opinion might be our own .

Real-World Consequences

This isn't just theoretical hand-wringing. There are tangible consequences when free speech gets squashed. Just look at some specific incidents. In 2016, DePaul University banned Ben Shapiro from its campus, citing security concerns after previous protests against his events turned violent. This decision followed a May 2016 event where Shapiro was escorted off campus by security after students disrupted his speech by storming the stage and shouting him down.

And then there's Jordan Peterson, whose 2017 speech at McMaster University was drowned out by relentless chanting and noise from protesters wielding air horns and megaphones. Peterson, known for his criticism of political correctness and compelled speech, was invited to discuss the implications of Bill C-16. Instead of a lively debate, the event devolved into chaos, forcing Peterson to abandon his lecture.

Such incidents create an environment where students learn that might makes right, and shouting down opposition is preferable to engaging with it. The result? An entire generation grows up with a skewed understanding of what free speech entails. According to a 2017 survey by the Brookings Institution, 51% of college students believe that it is acceptable to shout down a speaker to prevent them from speaking. Instead of robust debates, we get ideological monologues, where only the "correct" viewpoint is tolerated.

This erosion of free speech on campuses reflects broader societal trends. The National Coalition Against Censorship (NCAC) reported that in 2018 alone, there were over 100 attempts to disinvite speakers from college campuses due to their controversial views. These actions don't just stifle the speakers but also deprive students of the opportunity to hear and challenge differing perspectives, essential for intellectual growth and democracy.

The Data Doesn't Lie

Statistics back this up. A 2018 survey by FIRE found that 30% of college students believe it's acceptable to shout down a speaker to prevent them from speaking . Another study from the Brookings Institution revealed that 19% of students think violence is an accep'able response to "offensive" speech . These numbers paint a bleak picture of the current state of free expression on campuses.

It Doesn't Take a Genius...

So, just between you and me; as the only genius around, I'm going to boil it down for you. Political correctness, in its extreme form, becomes a muzzle on free speech. It's like playing "Simon Says," but with the threat of expulsion if you don't follow the arbitrary rules. To safeguard our ability to express diverse opinions, we must push back against these trends. After all, it doesn't take a genius to realize that without the freedom to speak our minds, we might as well be living in a giant echo chamber.

Who knew that defending free speech could be so politically correct—literally? Now it's your turn to be the smartest person in the room. Go forth and use your newfound wisdom to enlighten your less-informed friends. And remember, it's not just about being right; it's about ensuring that everyone has the right to be heard.

Undeniable Facts

1. **Historical Origins of Political Correctness**
   - Political correctness (PC) traces back to the early 20th century, linked to Marxist theory. It gained mainstream attention in the 1980s and 1990s in the U.S., primarily as a way to promote inclusive language and behaviors.

2. **Notable Incidents of Free Speech Suppression**
   - In 2017, Evergreen State College faced national scrutiny when protests erupted against Professor Bret Weinstein for questioning a campus event that asked white students to leave for a day. The situation escalated to violent threats and

campus lockdowns.

- In 2020, a New York Times opinion editor resigned after backlash for publishing a controversial op-ed by Senator Tom Cotton advocating for military intervention in protests.
- In 2019, Harvard University faced backlash after rescinding a fellowship invitation to Chelsea Manning, a whistleblower, following criticism from some faculty and alumni, sparking debates about academic freedom and free speech.
- In 2018, the University of California, Berkeley, spent approximately $600,000 on security for a speech by conservative commentator Ben Shapiro, following violent protests against previous speakers and raising concerns about the cost of protecting free speech.
- In 2021, the University of Edinburgh faced controversy for canceling a screening of the documentary "Adult Human Female," citing concerns about the film's stance on transgender issues, which led to debates on campus about censorship and academic freedom.

3. **Quotes About the Dangers of Limiting Free Speech**
   - "If liberty means anything at all, it means the right to tell people what they do not want to hear." – George Orwell
   - "Freedom is never more than one generation away from extinction." – Ronald Reagan

4. **Surprising Statistics on Free Speech Restrictions**
   - A 2018 survey by Gallup found that 61% of college students feel the climate on their campus prevents people from saying things they believe because others might find them offensive.
   - According to a 2021 Knight Foundation report, 68% of students say the campus climate stifles free expression.
   - A 2020 survey by the Foundation for Individual Rights in Education (FIRE) found that 60% of students believe that their college or university should be a place where all speech, even offensive speech, is protected.
   - The 2022 Campus Expression Survey by the Cato Institute

revealed that 62% of students agree that the political climate prevents them from saying things they believe because others might find them offens

- A 2019 study by the Higher Education Research Institute found that 74% of students agreed that colleges should expose students to all types of speech and viewpoints, even if they are offensive or biased.

5. **Fun Facts About Notable Free Speech Advocates**
    - John Stuart Mill, one of the earliest proponents of free speech, argued in his 1859 work "On Liberty" that silencing an opinion is an injustice to humanity.
    - Voltaire is famously (though perhaps apocryphally) quoted as saying, "I disapprove of what you say, but I will defend to the death your right to say it."

6. **Key Legislative Bills Related to Free Speech**
    - The First Amendment of the U.S. Constitution: Provides the foundational legal protections for free speech in the United States.
    - Bill C-16 (Canada, 2017): Amended the Canadian Human Rights Act to include gender identity and expression as prohibited grounds of discrimination, sparking debates about compelled speech.

7. **Dates and Outcomes of Major Free Speech Controversies**
    - 1977: The National Socialist Party of America v. Village of Skokie case, where the U.S. Supreme Court ruled in favor of allowing a Nazi group to march in a predominantly Jewish community.
    - 2014: Brendan Eich resigned as CEO of Mozilla after it was revealed he had donated to a campaign against same-sex marriage, raising questions about free speech and corporate responsibility.

8. **Notable Academics and Activists Involved in Free Speech Debates**
    - Noam Chomsky: Linguist and philosopher known for his strong defense of free speech, even for those he vehemently disagrees with.

- Nadine Strossen: Former ACLU president and law professor, renowned for her advocacy of free expression.

9. **Comparisons of Free Speech Policies in Different Countries**
    - United States: Strong protections under the First Amendment, though private institutions can set their own rules.
    - Germany: Strict laws against hate speech, including prohibitions on Holocaust denial and Nazi symbolism.
    - United Kingdom: Balances free speech with laws against hate speech and defamation, regulated by bodies like Ofcom.

10. **Case Studies of Specific Institutions and Their Free Speech Policies**
    - University of Chicago: Known for its strong stance on free expression, issuing the "Chicago Principles" which affirm the importance of free speech on campus.
    - Middlebury College: In 2017, Middlebury faced controversy when protests against Charles Murray's lecture turned violent, prompting debates on the limits of protest and free speech on campus.

The Influence of Media and Academia

Media and academia, the twin towers of public opinion, have an outsized influence on how we see the world. It's like having a TV remote that only has one working channel—no matter how much you click, you're stuck with the same show, the same storyline, and the same cast of characters. But is that the whole picture?

The Role of Media in Shaping Public Opinion

The media has a tremendous impact on cultural shifts and public opinion. From the news you watch in the morning to the social media feeds you scroll through at night, media is everywhere, feeding you a steady diet of what it wants you to believe. Studies from media bias research organizations like AllSides and Media Bias/Fact Check consistently show that media outlets often skew their reporting to fit specific ideological slants. This isn't just about what gets covered but how it's covered.

instance, the coordination of media narratives. During the 2020 U.S. presidential election, a study by the Media Research Center found that 92% of the media coverage of then-President Donald Trump was negative. In contrast, Joe Biden received predominantly positive coverage. Such skewed reporting creates an echo chamber effect, where viewers are continually exposed to the same perspectives, reinforcing their existing beliefs and suppressing opposing viewpoints.

It's almost as if the media got together for a big strategy meeting: "Alright team, how can we make sure everyone thinks the same way?" Just flip on your favorite news channel, and you'll find stories presented with the subtlety of a sledgehammer. A 2019 Pew Research Center survey showed that 69% of Americans feel that news organizations tend to favor one side in their reporting.

Then there's the magical world of social media, where algorithms work tirelessly to show you more of what you already agree with. Facebook, for instance, was found in a 2018 study by the Computational Propaganda Project to have played a significant role in spreading polarized content. It's like living in an echo chamber where the only voice you hear is your own, but with a chorus of agreeable nods.

But wait, there's more! A 2021 Reuters Institute Digital News Report revealed that 55% of respondents across 46 markets are concerned about distinguishing real news from fake news on the internet. With the media's trusty remote, stuck on the "One True Narrative" channel, is it any wonder we're all starting to think alike?

Academia: The Ivory Tower of Ideology

Academia isn't far behind in this game of shaping minds. Universities, once bastions of diverse thought and rigorous debate, have increasingly become echo chambers themselves. A 2018 survey by the National Association of Scholars found that liberal professors outnumber conservatives by a ratio of nearly 10 to 1 in the social sciences and humanities. Yes, you read that right—nearly 10 to 1. It's like a political monsoon season, but with no conservatives in sight.

This ideological homogeneity can lead to academic indoctrination, where students are subtly, and sometimes not-so-subtly, pushed towards adopting specific viewpoints. Imagine attending a "debate" where everyone's reading from the same script. How exciting.

For example, in 2017, a survey conducted by the Heterodox Academy revealed that 58% of students felt they had to self-censor in the classroom to avoid offending their professors or classmates. That's more than half the student body biting their tongues to stay on the "right" side of history. It's as if students are playing a never-ending game of "Don't Step on the Cracks," but instead of cracks, it's anyone's fragile ego.

This suppression of diverse viewpoints stifles debate and critical thinking, turning universities into places where only one narrative is accepted. A 2020 survey by the Foundation for Individual Rights in Education (FIRE) found that 60% of students believe their college should be a place where all speech, even offensive speech, is protected. Too bad their wishes seem to be as mythical as unicorns.

And let's not forget those brave souls who dare to invite controversial speakers to campus. The security costs alone could fund a small country's defense budget. For instance, the University of California, Berkeley, spent around $600,000 on security for a speech by conservative commentator Ben Shapiro in 2018. That's a hefty price tag just to hear someone challenge the status quo.

So here we are, stuck with academic institutions that preach the gospel of diversity while ensuring that intellectual diversity is about as welcome as a skunk at a garden party. Isn't higher education grand?

Media and Academia: The One-Channel Remote

Imagine if your TV remote only had one working channel—no matter how much you want to switch it up, you're stuck watching the same thing over and over. This analogy perfectly captures the current state of media and academia. Both institutions can promote specific ideologies while suppressing opposing viewpoints, creating a monoculture of thought.

Data from the Knight Foundation's 2021 report highlights that 68% of college students feel that their campus climate stifles free expression. Similarly, a 2020 study by the Cato Institute found that 62% of Americans say the political climate prevents them from saying things they believe because others might find them offensive. These statistics underline the pervasive influence of media and academia in promoting a one-sided narrative.

A Balanced Diet of Information

HOW TO UNDERSTAND LEFT-WING POLITICAL SPIN

It's clear that both media and academia play significant roles in shaping public opinion and cultural norms. However, their tendency to promote specific ideologies and suppress opposing viewpoints can lead to a skewed understanding of the world. As an unknown genius once said, "It doesn't take a genius to realize that a balanced diet of information is crucial for a healthy mind." So, next time you pick up that TV remote—or a textbook—remember that switching the channel, even metaphorically, is essential for true enlightenment.

Undeniable Facts

Trivia Points:

1. **Historical Examples of Media Influence on Public Opinion**
   - The 1898 Spanish-American War: Sensationalist reporting by newspapers like William Randolph Hearst's New York Journal and Joseph Pulitzer's New York World stirred public support for the war, exemplifying "yellow journalism."
   - The 1950s Red Scare: Media coverage fueled widespread fear of communism in the U.S., significantly impacting public opinion and government policies.

2. **Notable Cases of Academic Bias**
   - **The 2005 Ward Churchill controversy**: The University of Colorado professor faced backlash and eventual dismissal after making controversial statements about 9/11, raising debates about academic freedom and bias.
   - **The 2018 Evergreen State College protests**: Professor Bret Weinstein faced severe backlash and threats for criticizing a "Day of Absence" event that asked white students to leave campus.
   - **The 2017 University of Missouri Protests**: Student protests over racial issues led to the resignation of the university president and chancellor. The events sparked national debates about free speech, racial inequality, and the role of higher education in addressing social justice.
   - **The 2015 Yale University Halloween Email Controversy:**

A faculty member's email suggesting students should be free to choose their Halloween costumes led to significant protests and debates about free speech, cultural sensitivity, and academic freedom.

3. **Quotes About the Power of Media and Academia**
   - "The media's the most powerful entity on earth. They have the power to make the innocent guilty and to make the guilty innocent, and that's power." – Malcolm X
   - "Education is the most powerful weapon which you can use to change the world." – Nelson Mandela

4. **Surprising Statistics on Media Ownership and Bias**
   - As of 2021, six corporations control about 90% of the U.S. media, including Comcast, Disney, AT&T, Sony, Fox, and ViacomCBS.
   - A 2019 survey by Pew Research Center found that 64% of Americans believe fake news has caused a great deal of confusion about basic facts of current events.
   - A 2020 study by Gallup and the Knight Foundation found that 86% of Americans see a significant amount of bias in news coverage, and 49% say the media is very biased.
   - According to a 2021 report by Edelman, trust in traditional media hit an all-time low, with only 46% of people globally trusting the media.

5. **Fun Facts About Influential Media Figures**
   - **Oprah Winfrey**, one of the most influential media figures, turned her talk show into a platform for social change, impacting millions of viewers' perspectives on various issues.
   - **Rupert Murdoch**, founder of News Corporation, owns numerous media outlets worldwide, significantly influencing public opinion through his media empire.
   - **Walter Cronkite**: Known as "the most trusted man in America," Cronkite was a pioneering news anchor for CBS Evening News. His reporting on events like the Vietnam War and the Watergate scandal had a profound influence on

public opinion and American journalism.

- **Arianna Huffington**: Co-founder of The Huffington Post, Huffington has been a significant figure in digital media. Her platform has influenced public discourse on politics, culture, and lifestyle, becoming one of the most visited news sites globally.

6. **Key Legislative Bills Related to Media and Academic Freedom**
   - The First Amendment of the U.S. Constitution: Guarantees freedom of speech and press, providing the foundation for media and academic freedom.
   - The Higher Education Act of 1965: Includes provisions to promote academic freedom and prevent political interference in education.

7. **Dates and Outcomes of Major Media Controversies**
   - **2004**: CBS News aired a report questioning President George W. Bush's military service, leading to the "Rathergate" scandal and the resignation of anchor Dan Rather.
   - **2016**: The release of the "Access Hollywood" tape, where Donald Trump made controversial comments, significantly impacted the 2016 presidential election's media coverage.
   - **2019:** Actor Jussie Smollett reported an alleged hate crime, which later unraveled as a hoax. The media's initial widespread support and subsequent backlash highlighted issues of bias and credibility in news reporting.
   - **2013:** Rolling Stone published an article about an alleged gang rape at the University of Virginia, which was later discredited. The incident led to legal consequences and significant scrutiny of journalistic standards and verification processes.
   - **2003: The New York Times Jayson Blair Scandal**: Reporter Jayson Blair was found to have fabricated and plagiarized numerous stories, leading to his resignation and a broader discussion about ethics and oversight in journalism.

8. **Notable Academics Known for Their Influence on Public Opinion**
    - **Noam Chomsky**: A prominent linguist and political activist, Chomsky has been a vocal critic of media and government policies, influencing public discourse.
    - **Jordan Peterson**: A psychology professor whose views on political correctness and free speech have sparked widespread debate and garnered a large following.
    - **Allan Bloom**: A philosopher and author of "The Closing of the American Mind," Bloom critiqued higher education and its departure from classical liberal education principles. His work sparked debates about the purpose and direction of university education in America.
    - **Cornel West**: A philosopher, political activist, and public intellectual, West is known for his work on race, class, and justice. His books and public appearances have made him a prominent figure in discussions about social issues and academic freedom.
    - **Camille Paglia**: A professor and cultural critic known for her outspoken views on feminism, art, and popular culture. Paglia has been a significant influence in debates about gender, identity politics, and the role of academia in society.

9. **Comparisons of Media Bias in Different Countries**
    - United States: Known for a highly polarized media landscape, with significant ideological differences between outlets like Fox News and MSNBC.
    - United Kingdom: The BBC is often seen as more neutral, but there are still notable biases in other outlets like The Guardian and The Daily Mail.
    - Russia: State-controlled media like RT promotes the government's viewpoints, with limited space for dissenting opinions.

10. **Case Studies of Specific Media and Academic Institutions and Their Influence on Culture**

- ○ Harvard University: Known for its influential faculty and alumni, Harvard has played a significant role in shaping public policy and opinion through its research and public intellectuals.
- ○ The New York Times: As one of the most respected newspapers globally, The New York Times has a significant impact on public discourse, often setting the agenda for other media outlets.

14 - Cultural Shifts and Censorship

The term political correctness, which aims to create a society of inclusivity and kindness, often has unintended consequences that result in spectacular failures. Originally designed to protect individuals' emotions and foster a peaceful environment, it has now transformed into the playground bully, relentlessly silencing anyone who dares to deviate from conventional norms.

The PC Police: Stifling Open Dialogue

Imagine a game of "Simon Says" where "Simon" is an overly sensitive hall monitor who takes offense at the slightest hesitation. Go against the norm, and you'll be met with the fury of those who adhere to political correctness. The original intention was noble: to create a society where the sights and sounds of respect fill the air, making everyone feel valued. Yet in reality, it frequently constrains open dialogue and the sharing of diverse perspectives. When you're constantly worried about saying the "wrong" thing, your words lose their meaning and become empty.

Campus Craziness: The Free Speech Fiasco

Let's dive into the battlegrounds of political correctness: college campuses. These supposed bastions of free thought are now the epicenters of speech suppression. Remember when universities were about exploring new ideas and challenging the status quo? Good times.

Today, we're dealing with "safe spaces" and speech codes that could make Orwell blush. Safe spaces were meant to be havens from hate, but they've turned into echo chambers where dissenting opinions are as welcome as a skunk at a garden party. And speech codes? They're the unspoken rules of "Simon Says," but this time, the punishment for missteps is real.

For instance, take the deplatforming of controversial speakers like Ben Shapiro and Jordan Peterson. These guys are hardly the boogeymen of free speech, yet their mere presence on campus triggers protests that resemble a medieval witch hunt. According to the Foundation for Individual Rights in Education (FIRE), over half of U.S. colleges maintain policies that substantially restrict freedom of speech . The American Civil Liberties Union (ACLU) has also raised alarms about this trend, noting that true free speech includes protecting speech we don't like, because one day, that unpopular opinion might be our own .

Real-World Consequences

This isn't just theoretical hand-wringing. There are tangible consequences when free speech gets squashed. Just look at some specific incidents. In 2016, DePaul University banned Ben Shapiro from its campus, citing security concerns after previous protests against his events turned violent. This decision followed a May 2016 event where Shapiro was escorted off campus by security after students disrupted his speech by storming the stage and shouting him down.

And then there's Jordan Peterson, whose 2017 speech at McMaster University was drowned out by relentless chanting and noise from protesters wielding air horns and megaphones. Peterson, known for his criticism of political correctness and compelled speech, was invited to discuss the implications of Bill C-16. Instead of a lively debate, the event devolved into chaos, forcing Peterson to abandon his lecture.

Such incidents create an environment where students learn that might makes right, and shouting down opposition is preferable to engaging with it. The result? An entire generation grows up with a skewed understanding of what free speech entails. According to a 2017 survey by the Brookings Institution, 51% of college students believe that it is acceptable to shout down a speaker to prevent them from speaking. Instead of robust debates, we get ideological monologues, where only the "correct" viewpoint is tolerated.

This erosion of free speech on campuses reflects broader societal trends. The National Coalition Against Censorship (NCAC) reported that in 2018 alone, there were over 100 attempts to disinvite speakers from college campuses due to their controversial views. These actions don't just stifle the speakers but also deprive students of the opportunity to hear and challenge differing perspectives, essential for intellectual growth and democracy.

The Data 'Doesn't Lie

Statistics back this up. A 2018 survey by FIRE found that 30% of college students believe it's acceptable to shout down a speaker to prevent them from speaking . Another study from the Brookings Institution revealed that 19% of students think violence is an accep'able response to "offensive" speech . These numbers paint a bleak picture of the current state of free expression on campuses.

It Doesn't Take a Genius...

So, just between you and me; as the only genius around, I'm going to boil it down for you. Political correctness, in its extreme form, becomes a muzzle on free speech. It's like playing "Simon Says," but with the threat of expulsion if you don't follow the arbitrary rules. To safeguard our ability to express diverse opinions, we must push back against these trends. After all, it doesn't take a genius to realize that without the freedom to speak our minds, we might as well be living in a giant echo chamber.

Who knew that defending free speech could be so politically correct—literally? Now it's your turn to be the smartest person in the room. Go forth and use your newfound wisdom to enlighten your less-informed friends. And remember, it's not just about being right; it's about ensuring that everyone has the right to be heard.

Undeniable Facts

1. **Historical Origins of Political Correctness**
   ○ Political correctness (PC) traces back to the early 20th century, linked to Marxist theory. It gained mainstream attention in the 1980s and 1990s in the U.S., primarily as a way to promote inclusive language and behaviors.

2. **Notable Incidents of Free Speech Suppression**
   ○ In 2017, Evergreen State College faced national scrutiny when protests erupted against Professor Bret Weinstein for questioning a campus event that asked white students to leave for a day. The situation escalated to violent threats and

campus lockdowns.

- In 2020, a New York Times opinion editor resigned after backlash for publishing a controversial op-ed by Senator Tom Cotton advocating for military intervention in protests.
- In 2019, Harvard University faced backlash after rescinding a fellowship invitation to Chelsea Manning, a whistleblower, following criticism from some faculty and alumni, sparking debates about academic freedom and free speech.
- In 2018, the University of California, Berkeley, spent approximately $600,000 on security for a speech by conservative commentator Ben Shapiro, following violent protests against previous speakers and raising concerns about the cost of protecting free speech.
- In 2021, the University of Edinburgh faced controversy for canceling a screening of the documentary "Adult Human Female," citing concerns about the film's stance on transgender issues, which led to debates on campus about censorship and academic freedom.

3. **Quotes About the Dangers of Limiting Free Speech**
   - "If liberty means anything at all, it means the right to tell people what they do not want to hear." – George Orwell
   - "Freedom is never more than one generation away from extinction." – Ronald Reagan

4. **Surprising Statistics on Free Speech Restrictions**
   - A 2018 survey by Gallup found that 61% of college students feel the climate on their campus prevents people from saying things they believe because others might find them offensive.
   - According to a 2021 Knight Foundation report, 68% of students say the campus climate stifles free expression.
   - A 2020 survey by the Foundation for Individual Rights in Education (FIRE) found that 60% of students believe that their college or university should be a place where all speech, even offensive speech, is protected.
   - The 2022 Campus Expression Survey by the Cato Institute

revealed that 62% of students agree that the political climate prevents them from saying things they believe because others might find them offens

- A 2019 study by the Higher Education Research Institute found that 74% of students agreed that colleges should expose students to all types of speech and viewpoints, even if they are offensive or biased.

5. **Fun Facts About Notable Free Speech Advocates**
   - John Stuart Mill, one of the earliest proponents of free speech, argued in his 1859 work "On Liberty" that silencing an opinion is an injustice to humanity.
   - Voltaire is famously (though perhaps apocryphally) quoted as saying, "I disapprove of what you say, but I will defend to the death your right to say it."

6. **Key Legislative Bills Related to Free Speech**
   - The First Amendment of the U.S. Constitution: Provides the foundational legal protections for free speech in the United States.
   - Bill C-16 (Canada, 2017): Amended the Canadian Human Rights Act to include gender identity and expression as prohibited grounds of discrimination, sparking debates about compelled speech.

7. **Dates and Outcomes of Major Free Speech Controversies**
   - 1977: The National Socialist Party of America v. Village of Skokie case, where the U.S. Supreme Court ruled in favor of allowing a Nazi group to march in a predominantly Jewish community.
   - 2014: Brendan Eich resigned as CEO of Mozilla after it was revealed he had donated to a campaign against same-sex marriage, raising questions about free speech and corporate responsibility.

8. **Notable Academics and Activists Involved in Free Speech Debates**
   - Noam Chomsky: Linguist and philosopher known for his strong defense of free speech, even for those he vehemently disagrees with.

- ○ Nadine Strossen: Former ACLU president and law professor, renowned for her advocacy of free expression.

9. **Comparisons of Free Speech Policies in Different Countries**
   - ○ United States: Strong protections under the First Amendment, though private institutions can set their own rules.
   - ○ Germany: Strict laws against hate speech, including prohibitions on Holocaust denial and Nazi symbolism.
   - ○ United Kingdom: Balances free speech with laws against hate speech and defamation, regulated by bodies like Ofcom.

10. **Case Studies of Specific Institutions and Their Free Speech Policies**
    - ○ University of Chicago: Known for its strong stance on free expression, issuing the "Chicago Principles" which affirm the importance of free speech on campus.
    - ○ Middlebury College: In 2017, Middlebury faced controversy when protests against Charles Murray's lecture turned violent, prompting debates on the limits of protest and free speech on campus.

The Influence of Media and Academia

Media and academia, the twin towers of public opinion, have an outsized influence on how we see the world. It's like having a TV remote that only has one working channel—no matter how much you click, you're stuck with the same show, the same storyline, and the same cast of characters. But is that the whole picture?

The Role of Media in Shaping Public Opinion

The media has a tremendous impact on cultural shifts and public opinion. From the news you watch in the morning to the social media feeds you scroll through at night, media is everywhere, feeding you a steady diet of what it wants you to believe. Studies from media bias research organizations like AllSides and Media Bias/Fact Check consistently show that media outlets often skew their reporting to fit specific ideological slants. This isn't just about what gets covered but how it's covered.

Take, for instance, the coordination of media narratives. During the 2020 U.S. presidential election, a study by the Media Research Center found that 92% of the media coverage of then-President Donald Trump was negative. In contrast, Joe Biden received predominantly positive coverage. Such skewed reporting creates an echo chamber effect, where viewers are continually exposed to the same perspectives, reinforcing their existing beliefs and suppressing opposing viewpoints.

It's almost as if the media got together for a big strategy meeting: "Alright team, how can we make sure everyone thinks the same way?" Just flip on your favorite news channel, and you'll find stories presented with the subtlety of a sledgehammer. A 2019 Pew Research Center survey showed that 69% of Americans feel that news organizations tend to favor one side in their reporting.

Then there's the magical world of social media, where algorithms work tirelessly to show you more of what you already agree with. Facebook, for instance, was found in a 2018 study by the Computational Propaganda Project to have played a significant role in spreading polarized content. It's like living in an echo chamber where the only voice you hear is your own, but with a chorus of agreeable nods.

But wait, there's more! A 2021 Reuters Institute Digital News Report revealed that 55% of respondents across 46 markets are concerned about distinguishing real news from fake news on the internet. With the media's trusty remote, stuck on the "One True Narrative" channel, is it any wonder we're all starting to think alike?

Academia: The Ivory Tower of Ideology

Academia isn't far behind in this game of shaping minds. Universities, once bastions of diverse thought and rigorous debate, have increasingly become echo chambers themselves. A 2018 survey by the National Association of Scholars found that liberal professors outnumber conservatives by a ratio of nearly 10 to 1 in the social sciences and humanities. Yes, you read that right—nearly 10 to 1. It's like a political monsoon season, but with no conservatives in sight.

This ideological homogeneity can lead to academic indoctrination, where students are subtly, and sometimes not-so-subtly, pushed towards adopting specific viewpoints. Imagine attending a "debate" where everyone's reading from the same script. How exciting.

For example, in 2017, a survey conducted by the Heterodox Academy revealed that 58% of students felt they had to self-censor in the classroom to avoid offending their professors or classmates. That's more than half the student body biting their tongues to stay on the "right" side of history. It's as if students are playing a never-ending game of "Don't Step on the Cracks," but instead of cracks, it's anyone's fragile ego.

This suppression of diverse viewpoints stifles debate and critical thinking, turning universities into places where only one narrative is accepted. A 2020 survey by the Foundation for Individual Rights in Education (FIRE) found that 60% of students believe their college should be a place where all speech, even offensive speech, is protected. Too bad their wishes seem to be as mythical as unicorns.

And let's not forget those brave souls who dare to invite controversial speakers to campus. The security costs alone could fund a small country's defense budget. For instance, the University of California, Berkeley, spent around $600,000 on security for a speech by conservative commentator Ben Shapiro in 2018. That's a hefty price tag just to hear someone challenge the status quo.

So here we are, stuck with academic institutions that preach the gospel of diversity while ensuring that intellectual diversity is about as welcome as a skunk at a garden party. Isn't higher education grand?

Media and Academia: The One-Channel Remote

Imagine if your TV remote only had one working channel—no matter how much you want to switch it up, you're stuck watching the same thing over and over. This analogy perfectly captures the current state of media and academia. Both institutions can promote specific ideologies while suppressing opposing viewpoints, creating a monoculture of thought.

Data from the Knight Foundation's 2021 report highlights that 68% of college students feel that their campus climate stifles free expression. Similarly, a 2020 study by the Cato Institute found that 62% of Americans say the political climate prevents them from saying things they believe because others might find them offensive. These statistics underline the pervasive influence of media and academia in promoting a one-sided narrative.

A Balanced Diet of Information

It's clear that both media and academia play significant roles in shaping public opinion and cultural norms. However, their tendency to promote specific ideologies and suppress opposing viewpoints can lead to a skewed understanding of the world. As an unknown genius once said, "It doesn't take a genius to realize that a balanced diet of information is crucial for a healthy mind." So, next time you pick up that TV remote—or a textbook—remember that switching the channel, even metaphorically, is essential for true enlightenment.

Undeniable Facts

Trivia Points:

1. **Historical Examples of Media Influence on Public Opinion**
   - The 1898 Spanish-American War: Sensationalist reporting by newspapers like William Randolph Hearst's New York Journal and Joseph Pulitzer's New York World stirred public support for the war, exemplifying "yellow journalism."
   - The 1950s Red Scare: Media coverage fueled widespread fear of communism in the U.S., significantly impacting public opinion and government policies.

2. **Notable Cases of Academic Bias**
   - **The 2005 Ward Churchill controversy**: The University of Colorado professor faced backlash and eventual dismissal after making controversial statements about 9/11, raising debates about academic freedom and bias.
   - **The 2018 Evergreen State College protests**: Professor Bret Weinstein faced severe backlash and threats for criticizing a "Day of Absence" event that asked white students to leave campus.
   - **The 2017 University of Missouri Protests**: Student protests over racial issues led to the resignation of the university president and chancellor. The events sparked national debates about free speech, racial inequality, and the role of higher education in addressing social justice.
   - **The 2015 Yale University Halloween Email Controversy:**

A faculty member's email suggesting students should be free to choose their Halloween costumes led to significant protests and debates about free speech, cultural sensitivity, and academic freedom.

3. **Quotes About the Power of Media and Academia**
   - "The media's the most powerful entity on earth. They have the power to make the innocent guilty and to make the guilty innocent, and that's power." – Malcolm X
   - "Education is the most powerful weapon which you can use to change the world." – Nelson Mandela

4. **Surprising Statistics on Media Ownership and Bias**
   - As of 2021, six corporations control about 90% of the U.S. media, including Comcast, Disney, AT&T, Sony, Fox, and ViacomCBS.
   - A 2019 survey by Pew Research Center found that 64% of Americans believe fake news has caused a great deal of confusion about basic facts of current events.
   - A 2020 study by Gallup and the Knight Foundation found that 86% of Americans see a significant amount of bias in news coverage, and 49% say the media is very biased.
   - According to a 2021 report by Edelman, trust in traditional media hit an all-time low, with only 46% of people globally trusting the media.

5. **Fun Facts About Influential Media Figures**
   - **Oprah Winfrey**, one of the most influential media figures, turned her talk show into a platform for social change, impacting millions of viewers' perspectives on various issues.
   - **Rupert Murdoch**, founder of News Corporation, owns numerous media outlets worldwide, significantly influencing public opinion through his media empire.
   - **Walter Cronkite**: Known as "the most trusted man in America," Cronkite was a pioneering news anchor for CBS Evening News. His reporting on events like the Vietnam War and the Watergate scandal had a profound influence on

public opinion and American journalism.

- **Arianna Huffington**: Co-founder of The Huffington Post, Huffington has been a significant figure in digital media. Her platform has influenced public discourse on politics, culture, and lifestyle, becoming one of the most visited news sites globally.

6. **Key Legislative Bills Related to Media and Academic Freedom**
   - The First Amendment of the U.S. Constitution: Guarantees freedom of speech and press, providing the foundation for media and academic freedom.
   - The Higher Education Act of 1965: Includes provisions to promote academic freedom and prevent political interference in education.

7. **Dates and Outcomes of Major Media Controversies**
   - **2004**: CBS News aired a report questioning President George W. Bush's military service, leading to the "Rathergate" scandal and the resignation of anchor Dan Rather.
   - **2016**: The release of the "Access Hollywood" tape, where Donald Trump made controversial comments, significantly impacted the 2016 presidential election's media coverage.
   - **2019:** Actor Jussie Smollett reported an alleged hate crime, which later unraveled as a hoax. The media's initial widespread support and subsequent backlash highlighted issues of bias and credibility in news reporting.
   - **2013:** Rolling Stone published an article about an alleged gang rape at the University of Virginia, which was later discredited. The incident led to legal consequences and significant scrutiny of journalistic standards and verification processes.
   - **2003: The New York Times Jayson Blair Scandal:** Reporter Jayson Blair was found to have fabricated and plagiarized numerous stories, leading to his resignation and a broader discussion about ethics and oversight in journalism.

8. **Notable Academics Known for Their Influence on Public Opinion**
   - **Noam Chomsky**: A prominent linguist and political activist, Chomsky has been a vocal critic of media and government policies, influencing public discourse.
   - **Jordan Peterson**: A psychology professor whose views on political correctness and free speech have sparked widespread debate and garnered a large following.
   - **Allan Bloom**: A philosopher and author of "The Closing of the American Mind," Bloom critiqued higher education and its departure from classical liberal education principles. His work sparked debates about the purpose and direction of university education in America.
   - **Cornel West**: A philosopher, political activist, and public intellectual, West is known for his work on race, class, and justice. His books and public appearances have made him a prominent figure in discussions about social issues and academic freedom.
   - **Camille Paglia**: A professor and cultural critic known for her outspoken views on feminism, art, and popular culture. Paglia has been a significant influence in debates about gender, identity politics, and the role of academia in society.

9. **Comparisons of Media Bias in Different Countries**
   - United States: Known for a highly polarized media landscape, with significant ideological differences between outlets like Fox News and MSNBC.
   - United Kingdom: The BBC is often seen as more neutral, but there are still notable biases in other outlets like The Guardian and The Daily Mail.
   - Russia: State-controlled media like RT promotes the government's viewpoints, with limited space for dissenting opinions.

10. **Case Studies of Specific Media and Academic Institutions and Their Influence on Culture**

- Harvard University: Known for its influential faculty and alumni, Harvard has played a significant role in shaping public policy and opinion through its research and public intellectuals.
- The New York Times: As one of the most respected newspapers globally, The New York Times has a significant impact on public discourse, often setting the agenda for other media outlets.

15: The Global Perspective

Liberal foreign policies, often aimed at promoting peace and stability, sometimes end up creating more chaos than they prevent. It's like playing a game of Risk without understanding the rules—expect a mess on the global stage.

Notable Foreign Policy Mistakes Under Liberal Administrations

Let's dive into some of the most significant blunders. One of the standout examples is the Iran nuclear deal, formally known as the Joint Comprehensive Plan of Action (JCPOA), orchestrated under President Obama in 2015. The idea was to curb Iran's nuclear capabilities in exchange for lifting economic sanctions. Critics argue that the deal provided Iran with financial resources while only temporarily limiting its nuclear ambitions. In fact, according to the Council on Foreign Relations, the deal's sunset clauses would eventually allow Iran to resume its nuclear program, potentially destabilizing the Middle East in the long run.

Then there's the hasty withdrawal from Afghanistan in 2021. President Biden's administration oversaw the chaotic exit, which left the Taliban seizing control of the country faster than you could say "nation-building." The rapid fall of Kabul not only tarnished U.S. credibility but also left thousands of Afghans, who had supported American efforts, in grave danger. A report by the Special Inspector General for Afghanistan Reconstruction (SIGAR) highlighted the numerous missteps and the resulting humanitarian crisis.

The handling of the Libyan crisis is another glaring example. In 2011, the Obama administration, supported by NATO allies, intervened in Libya to topple Muammar Gaddafi. While the Authorization for Use of Military Force (AUMF) in Libya aimed to prevent a humanitarian disaster, it inadvertently plunged the country into a prolonged civil war, creating a power vacuum that extremist groups eagerly filled. The aftermath saw Libya becoming a breeding ground for terrorism and human trafficking, contributing to regional instability.

Consequences on International Relations and Global Stability

These policies didn't just cause local upheavals; they had far-reaching impacts on international relations and global stability. The Iran deal, for instance, strained U.S. relations with key allies like Israel and Saudi Arabia, who viewed the agreement as a direct threat to their security. The fallout from Afghanistan's withdrawal was felt globally, with allies questioning the reliability of U.S. commitments.

The Libyan intervention had Europe facing a massive migration crisis, with thousands of refugees fleeing the conflict. According to the International Organization for Migration, the Mediterranean became one of the deadliest migration routes, with over 3,000 deaths reported in 2015 alone. The instability in Libya also had a ripple effect, exacerbating conflicts in neighboring countries like Mali and Nigeria.

Legislative Examples and Data

Specific legislative actions underpin these policies, often with the precision of a bull in a china shop. Take the Joint Comprehensive Plan of Action (JCPOA), for instance. Signed in July 2015, the deal was lauded as a breakthrough in preventing nuclear proliferation. The goal was to curb Iran's nuclear program in exchange for lifting crippling economic sanctions. However, critics argue that the deal, set to expire in stages over a period of 10 to 15 years, was akin to giving a temporary hall pass to a notorious troublemaker. The U.S. State Department's own 2018 report raised concerns about Iran's compliance, noting instances where Iran exceeded the allowed limits of enriched uranium.

The debate over the JCPOA's effectiveness is well-documented. The Council on Foreign Relations and international relations journals have churned out analysis after analysis, often concluding that the deal was a band-aid on a bullet wound. Critics point out that by the time the sunset clauses kick in, Iran could have advanced its nuclear technology enough to become an unstoppable force in the region. In short, it's like putting a cork in a volcano and hoping it doesn't blow.

Then there's the Authorization for Use of Military Force (AUMF) in Libya, passed by Congress in March 2011. This legislative green light led to a NATO intervention that toppled Muammar Gaddafi, creating what can only be described as a political game of Jenga. Pull out one piece, and the whole structure collapses. Post-Gaddafi Libya descended into chaos, with various factions vying for control. By 2014, Libya had split into two rival governments, and the violence and instability allowed extremist groups like ISIS to gain a foothold.

The numbers paint a grim picture. A 2017 UN report estimated that over 200,000 people had been displaced by the ongoing conflict, and human rights organizations like Amnesty International have documented widespread abuses. The intervention, initially heralded as a humanitarian success, quickly morphed into a case study of how not to conduct foreign policy.

In both cases, the lack of robust post-conflict planning was glaring. The JCPOA didn't account for what would happen once Iran resumed its nuclear activities, while the AUMF in Libya overlooked the complexities of nation-building in a fractured society. It's like planning a wedding and forgetting about the marriage—sure, the ceremony might be spectacular, but what happens afterward is a complete mess.

So, while these legislative actions were crafted with the best intentions, they often fell short in execution. It doesn't take a genius to see that sometimes, a bit more foresight could have saved a lot of trouble. But then again, in the world of liberal foreign policy, hindsight is 20/20, and foresight is apparently optional.

Liberal foreign policy often resembles a game of Risk played by someone who hasn't read the rules. The initial moves might seem strategic, but as the game progresses, it's clear that chaos is just around the corner. Borders shift unpredictably, allies become enemies, and in the end, everyone is left scrambling to pick up the pieces.

As shocking as it sounds, the intentions behind liberal foreign policies might be noble. But the outcomes often tell a different story. From the Iran deal to Afghanistan and Libya, these decisions have left a trail of unintended consequences that continue to shape global dynamics. So next time you hear about a new diplomatic initiative, just remember: it doesn't take a genius to see that sometimes, understanding the rules can make all the difference.

Undeniable Facts

1. **Historical Examples of Liberal Foreign Policy Decisions**
   - **The 1978 Camp David Accords**: Brokered by President Jimmy Carter, this agreement aimed to establish peace between Egypt and Israel, demonstrating a significant liberal diplomatic achievement.
   - **The Marshall Plan (1948)**: Initiated by President Truman, this massive aid program helped rebuild Western Europe after World War II and was a hallmark of liberal internationalism.

- **The Iran Nuclear Deal (JCPOA) (2015):** Negotiated by President Barack Obama's administration, this agreement aimed to limit Iran's nuclear capabilities in exchange for lifting economic sanctions. While controversial, it was seen as a major diplomatic effort to prevent nuclear proliferation through negotiation rather than military action.
- **The Good Friday Agreement (1998):** Brokered by President Bill Clinton and British Prime Minister Tony Blair, this peace agreement aimed to end the conflict in Northern Ireland. It was a significant diplomatic achievement and a hallmark of liberal efforts to resolve longstanding conflicts through negotiation.

2. **Notable Foreign Policy Blunders and Their Impacts**
   - **The Iran Hostage Crisis (1979-1981):** President Carter's handling of the crisis, including the failed rescue mission, led to significant political and diplomatic fallout.
   - **The 2011 Libyan Intervention:** Authorized by President Obama, the NATO-led mission to topple Muammar Gaddafi led to ongoing civil war and regional instability.
   - **The Vietnam War Escalation (1965-1973):** Under President Lyndon B. Johnson, the significant escalation of U.S. military involvement in Vietnam led to a protracted and unpopular conflict with severe human and financial costs, ultimately resulting in a withdrawal and a tarnished legacy for the administration.
   - **The Bay of Pigs Invasion (1961):** Authorized by President John F. Kennedy, this failed attempt to overthrow Fidel Castro's government in Cuba led to international embarrassment and strained U.S.-Cuban relations for decades.
   - **The Iraq Withdrawal (2011):** Initiated under President Obama, the complete withdrawal of U.S. troops from Iraq led to a power vacuum that contributed to the rise of ISIS

and significant regional instability, prompting critiques of the administration's strategy.

3. **Quotes About the Consequences of Liberal Foreign Policies**
    - "The road to hell is paved with good intentions." – An adage often cited to describe the unintended consequences of well-meaning policies.
    - "In the realm of diplomacy, clarity and consistency are key; without them, even the noblest of intentions can lead to chaos." – Former Secretary of State Henry Kissinger

4. **Surprising Statistics on the Outcomes of Specific Foreign Policy Decisions**
    - A 2021 report by the Watson Institute at Brown University found that the U.S. War on Terror has cost over $8 trillion and resulted in over 929,000 deaths, highlighting the long-term consequences of interventionist policies.
    - The Iran nuclear deal (JCPOA) provided Iran with an estimated $100 billion in sanctions relief, according to a 2015 report by the U.S. Treasury Department.
    - A 2019 report by the Special Inspector General for Afghanistan Reconstruction (SIGAR) revealed that over $19 billion of U.S. taxpayer money was lost to waste, fraud, and abuse in Afghanistan, highlighting the inefficiencies and challenges in nation-building efforts.
    - According to a 2017 study by the International Organization for Migration, the 2011 Libyan intervention led to over 600,000 migrants and refugees attempting to cross the Mediterranean, resulting in thousands of deaths and a significant humanitarian crisis.
    - A 2018 Pew Research Center survey found that 43% of Americans believe that U.S. involvement in foreign conflicts has made the country less safe, underscoring public skepticism about the benefits of interventionist foreign policies.

5. **Fun Facts About International Diplomatic Incidents**

- The Great Emu War (1932): An unusual example of foreign policy blunders, where Australia declared war on emus to control their population, leading to an embarrassing defeat.
- The Pig War (1859): A confrontation between the U.S. and the UK over the boundary in the San Juan Islands, triggered by the shooting of a pig.

6. **Key Legislative Bills Related to Foreign Policy**
   - The War Powers Resolution (1973): Limits the president's ability to engage in military action without congressional approval, reflecting liberal concerns about executive overreach.
   - The Foreign Assistance Act (1961): Launched the U.S. Agency for International Development (USAID) and aimed to promote social and economic development abroad.

7. **Dates and Outcomes of Major International Agreements**
   - The Paris Agreement (2015): A global pact to combat climate change, signed under President Obama, aimed at reducing carbon emissions and promoting sustainable development.
   - The Oslo Accords (1993): Facilitated by President Clinton, these agreements aimed to resolve the Israeli-Palestinian conflict but have faced significant challenges and criticisms.

8. **Notable Diplomats and Politicians Involved in Foreign Policy Blunders**
   - Madeleine Albright: As Secretary of State, she was a key architect of the NATO intervention in Kosovo, which faced both praise and criticism.
   - John Kerry: As Secretary of State, he played a pivotal role in negotiating the Iran nuclear deal, which remains controversial.

9. **Comparisons of Foreign Policy Approaches Between Liberal and Conservative Administrations**
   - Liberal administrations often emphasize multilateralism and diplomatic engagement, as seen in the Obama administration's approach to the Iran nuclear deal.

- ○ Conservative administrations may prioritize military strength and unilateral action, exemplified by the Bush administration's 2003 invasion of Iraq.

10. **Case Studies of Specific Countries Affected by Liberal Foreign Policies**
    - ○ **Afghanistan**: The withdrawal in 2021 under President Biden led to a rapid Taliban takeover, sparking debates about the long-term impact of U.S. involvement.
    - ○ **Libya:** The 2011 intervention led to ongoing conflict and instability, raising questions about the efficacy of humanitarian military interventions.
    - ○ **Iraq**: The 2003 invasion under President George W. Bush aimed to remove Saddam Hussein and eliminate weapons of mass destruction. The subsequent occupation and withdrawal in 2011 led to sectarian violence, the rise of ISIS, and ongoing instability, raising significant questions about the long-term consequences of military intervention.
    - ○ **Syria**: Under President Obama's administration, the U.S. initially supported Syrian rebels during the civil war but faced criticism for inconsistent policies and failure to prevent humanitarian disasters. The conflict continues to result in significant regional instability and a massive refugee crisis.

The Global Impact of Progressive Ideals

Progressive ideals are like tropical plants: they may thrive in their native environment, but try planting them in the Arctic, and you're in for a world of hurt. When it comes to exporting these well-intentioned policies worldwide, the results range from mildly amusing to downright disastrous.

How Progressive Policies Have Influenced Global Social and Economic Landscapes

Progressive policies often aim to improve the world, but when they leap from theory to practice on the global stage, they tend to trip over their own feet. Let's start with the Paris Agreement on climate change. Signed in 2016 with great fanfare, this treaty aimed to reduce global carbon emissions. Fast forward a few years, and we see the U.S. pulling out under President Trump, only to rejoin under President Biden. Meanwhile, global emissions continue to rise. The United Nations reported in 2020 that we're nowhere near meeting the targets set.

It's almost as if signing a piece of paper didn't magically fix the planet. Who knew?

The Spread of Environmental Policies

Take the Green New Deal, for example. The idea was to push for renewable energy and reduce reliance on fossil fuels.

Great in theory, right?

But then you have Germany, which decided to shut down its nuclear power plants post-Fukushima. The result? A 2019 study by the Fraunhofer Institute showed that Germany's carbon emissions barely budged, and the country ended up importing coal-generated electricity from Poland.

It's like trying to cure a headache by cutting off your head—slightly overkill and definitely not effective.

Social Justice Movements

Then we have the global spread of social justice movements. The U.S. exported its brand of identity politics to the world, resulting in some rather colorful outcomes.

In the UK, universities adopted speech codes and safe spaces with gusto. According to a 2021 report by the UK's Office for Students, these policies often stifled debate more than they protected students.

The irony is palpable—safe spaces so safe that they're intellectually barren.

Economic Redistribution Efforts

Let's not forget the economic redistribution efforts. Countries like Venezuela took the progressive playbook and ran with it. Implementing massive social welfare programs and nationalizing industries led to what can only be described as an economic apocalypse.

By 2021, the World Bank reported that Venezuela's inflation rate had hit an astronomical 2,355%, with citizens fleeing the country in droves.

Ah yes, the sweet smell of success.

The Paris Agreement, as noble as it sounds, is a prime example of how progressive ideals can flounder. Despite commitments to reduce emissions, a

2021 report by the International Energy Agency noted that coal use had surged back to pre-Paris levels. It's almost like the global economy didn't get the memo about going green.

International aid programs, heavily influenced by progressive policies, aim to lift countries out of poverty. Yet, according to a 2019 study by the Brookings Institution, many of these efforts lead to dependency rather than development. Countries receive aid but fail to build sustainable infrastructures. It's the difference between giving a man a fish and teaching him to fish—but progressive policies seem to favor flooding the market with free fish.

Spreading progressive ideals globally is like trying to plant tropical plants in the Arctic—well-intentioned but not always effective. The plants might look good for a day or two, but pretty soon, you're left with a bunch of frozen, dead foliage. Similarly, progressive policies often fail to take root in the complex, varied soils of global politics and economics.

What it all comes down to is this; while progressive ideals may come from a place of wanting to make the world better, their implementation often leaves much to be desired. And "much" is spelled S-H-I-T-L-O-A-D. From environmental policies that backfire to social justice movements that silence more than they liberate, the road to global improvement is paved with good intentions—and a lot of unintended consequences.

So next time you hear about the latest progressive initiative, just remember: it doesn't take a genius to see that tropical plants belong in the tropics, not the Arctic.

Undeniable Facts

1. **Historical Examples of Progressive Ideals Implemented Globally**
    -   **The Universal Declaration of Human Rights (1948):**
        Championed by Eleanor Roosevelt, this document set out
        fundamental human rights to be universally protected,
        embodying progressive ideals on a global scale.
    -   **The Kyoto Protocol (1997):** An international treaty aimed
        at reducing greenhouse gas emissions, reflecting global
        commitment to environmental sustainability and
        progressive climate policies.

- **The Montreal Protocol (1987):** An international treaty designed to phase out the production of substances that deplete the ozone layer. This agreement has been highly successful, with the UN reporting that over 98% of ozone-depleting substances have been eliminated globally.
- **The Convention on the Rights of the Child (1989):** Adopted by the United Nations General Assembly, this treaty aims to protect the rights of children worldwide, ensuring they have access to education, healthcare, and a safe environment, reflecting progressive ideals in child welfare and human rights.

2. **Notable International Agreements Influenced by Progressive Policies**

- **The Paris Agreement (2015):** A landmark international treaty aimed at combating climate change by limiting global warming to below 2 degrees Celsius.
- **The Global Compact for Migration (2018):** An agreement adopted by the United Nations to address migration issues, emphasizing human rights and progressive approaches to international migration.
- **The Sustainable Development Goals (SDGs) (2015):** Adopted by the United Nations, this set of 17 global goals aims to end poverty, protect the planet, and ensure prosperity for all by 2030. These goals reflect progressive ideals in environmental sustainability, social justice, and economic development.
- **The Biodiversity Convention (1992):** Formally known as the Convention on Biological Diversity, this international treaty focuses on the conservation of biological diversity, the sustainable use of its components, and the fair sharing of benefits arising from genetic resources. It embodies progressive environmental and sustainability goals.
- **The International Labour Organization's Decent Work**

Agenda (1999): This initiative aims to promote fair and safe working conditions, employment opportunities, and social protection for workers worldwide, reflecting progressive labor standards and human rights.

3. **Quotes About the Global Impact of Progressive Ideals**
    - "The future belongs to those who believe in the beauty of their dreams." – Eleanor Roosevelt
    - "Injustice anywhere is a threat to justice everywhere." – Martin Luther King Jr.

4. **Surprising Statistics on the Outcomes of International Progressive Policies**
    - According to the World Bank, global poverty rates have declined from 36% in 1990 to 10% in 2015, partly due to progressive international aid and development policies.
    - A 2020 report by the United Nations found that countries adhering to the Sustainable Development Goals (SDGs) showed a 20% increase in renewable energy capacity since 2015.
    - A 2018 report by the World Health Organization (WHO) found that global life expectancy increased by 5.5 years between 2000 and 2016, largely due to improved access to healthcare and progressive public health initiatives.
    - A 2019 study by the International Renewable Energy Agency (IRENA) revealed that the cost of renewable energy technologies, such as solar and wind, has dropped by over 80% since 2010, significantly accelerating their adoption worldwide and reflecting the impact of progressive energy policies.

5. **Fun Facts About Global Social Justice Movements**
    - The #MeToo movement, which began in the U.S., has spread to over 85 countries, highlighting global issues of gender inequality and sexual harassment.
    - The global Climate Strike movement, inspired by Greta Thunberg, has mobilized millions of young people in over

150 countries to demand climate action.

- ◦ The Black Lives Matter movement, originating in the U.S. in 2013, has spread to numerous countries worldwide, bringing attention to issues of racial injustice and police brutality on a global scale.
- ◦ The Fridays for Future movement, also inspired by Greta Thunberg, has led to weekly climate strikes in over 100 countries, advocating for urgent environmental policies and raising awareness about the climate crisis.

6. **Key International Treaties and Agreements**
   - ◦ **The Rome Statute (1998):** Established the International Criminal Court (ICC) to prosecute individuals for genocide, crimes against humanity, and war crimes.
   - ◦ **The Convention on the Elimination of All Forms of Discrimination Against Women (CEDAW) (1979):** An international treaty aimed at promoting gender equality and women's rights.
   - ◦ **The Convention on the Rights of Persons with Disabilities (CRPD) (2006):** This international treaty aims to protect the rights and dignity of persons with disabilities, ensuring they have equal access to education, employment, and social participation.
   - ◦ **The Treaty on the Non-Proliferation of Nuclear Weapons (NPT) (1968):** This treaty seeks to prevent the spread of nuclear weapons and promote the peaceful use of nuclear energy, reflecting progressive ideals of global security and disarmament.

7. **Dates and Outcomes of Major Global Policy Initiatives**
   - ◦ **The Millennium Development Goals (MDGs) (2000-2015):** A set of eight international development goals that resulted in significant progress in reducing extreme poverty and improving health and education outcomes worldwide.
   - ◦ **The Sustainable Development Goals (SDGs)**

(2015-present): A collection of 17 global goals designed to achieve a better and more sustainable future for all by 2030.

- **The Doha Declaration (2015)**: Adopted at the 13th United Nations Congress on Crime Prevention and Criminal Justice, this declaration emphasizes the integration of crime prevention and criminal justice into the wider United Nations agenda, promoting social and economic development and the rule of law.
- **The New Urban Agenda (2016)**: Adopted at the United Nations Conference on Housing and Sustainable Urban Development (Habitat III), this agenda provides a roadmap for sustainable urbanization and aims to make cities inclusive, safe, resilient, and sustainable.

8. **Notable International Figures Promoting Progressive Ideals**
   - Malala Yousafzai: Nobel Peace Prize laureate and advocate for girls' education and women's rights globally.
   - António Guterres: The current UN Secretary-General, known for his efforts to address climate change, humanitarian crises, and promote sustainable development.

9. **Comparisons of Global Policies Influenced by Progressive and Conservative Ideologies**
   - **Progressive policies**, such as those seen in Scandinavian countries, emphasize social welfare, environmental sustainability, and inclusivity. For example, Norway's comprehensive social safety nets and green energy initiatives.
   - **Conservative policies**, like those in the United States under various administrations, often focus on economic deregulation, military strength, and traditional values. For instance, the U.S. withdrawal from the Paris Agreement under President Trump.
   - **Canada's Universal Healthcare System**: Emphasizes the progressive value of providing healthcare to all citizens, ensuring that everyone has access to medical services regardless of their financial situation. This system is funded

through taxes and is a cornerstone of Canada's social welfare policies.

- **United Kingdom's Brexit (2016)**: Aimed at regaining national sovereignty and reducing the influence of the European Union on British laws and policies. This decision emphasized conservative values of national independence, economic deregulation, and control over immigration.
- **Germany's Energiewende Initiative**: A comprehensive policy aimed at transitioning Germany to a sustainable energy system. This initiative focuses on increasing the use of renewable energy, improving energy efficiency, and reducing greenhouse gas emissions, reflecting progressive ideals of environmental sustainability.
- **Australia's Immigration Policies Under Prime Minister Tony Abbott**: Focused on strict border control measures and reducing illegal immigration. Policies such as Operation Sovereign Borders were implemented to deter asylum seekers and emphasize national security and sovereignty, aligning with conservative ideals.

10. **Case Studies of Specific Countries Influenced by Progressive Policies**
    - **Germany**: Known for its progressive environmental policies, Germany has invested heavily in renewable energy, leading to nearly 40% of its electricity coming from renewable sources as of 2019.
    - **New Zealand**: Under Prime Minister Jacinda Ardern, the country has implemented progressive policies on climate change, social welfare, and gender equality, making it a leading example of modern progressive governance.
    - **Sweden**: Renowned for its progressive social policies, Sweden offers extensive parental leave, universal healthcare, and free higher education. As of 2020, Sweden's investment in renewable energy sources has led to over 54% of its total

energy consumption coming from renewables.

- **Costa Rica**: Celebrated for its commitment to environmental sustainability, Costa Rica generates nearly 98% of its electricity from renewable sources and has set ambitious goals to become carbon neutral by 2050. The country also prioritizes social welfare and healthcare, reflecting its progressive governance.

- **Denmark**: Known for its robust social safety nets and environmental initiatives, Denmark is a leader in wind energy, producing 47% of its electricity from wind power as of 2019. The country also offers free education, universal healthcare, and generous parental leave, embodying progressive policies in various sectors.

16 - Real-Life Success Stories from Red States

Conservative Policies Fueling Economic Powerhouses

Ever heard the phrase, "As an unknown genius, I can assure you..."? Well, as the only genius in this narrative, let me introduce you to some shining examples of economic brilliance from America's red states. Buckle up as we reveal how conservative policies have transformed these regions into economic powerhouses, effectively making them the poster children for fiscal success.

The Texas Tech Boom

Texas, my dear genius wannabe, isn't just about cowboys and BBQ. This state has become a tech titan, rivaling even Silicon Valley. Companies like Tesla, Oracle, and Hewlett Packard Enterprise have packed their bags and moved to Texas. Why? Low taxes, deregulation, and a business-friendly environment.

The Lone Star State offers tax incentives that make CEOs salivate. For instance, the Texas Enterprise Fund (TEF) provides grants to companies that create jobs and invest in the state. This approach has turned Texas into a magnet for innovation and entrepreneurship.

Tennessee's Manufacturing Resurgence

Remember when Tennessee was just known for country music and Elvis? Well, hold onto your blue suede shoes because the Volunteer State is experiencing a manufacturing renaissance. Tennessee's right-to-work laws make it an attractive destination for manufacturers. Companies like Nissan and Volkswagen have set up shop here, creating thousands of jobs. It's like watching a well-oiled machine in action—efficient, productive, and churning out economic success.

Florida: The Sunshine State's Economic Growth

Florida isn't just about beaches and retirees anymore. With no state income tax, it's a paradise for businesses and individuals alike. The economic growth in Florida is a testament to the power of conservative policies. The state has seen a surge in population and job creation, particularly in industries like tourism, construction, and aerospace. Legislative measures, such as tax incentives for businesses and investments in infrastructure, have paved the way for sustained economic prosperity.

Data Speaks Volumes

Let's not just take my genius word for it—let's look at the numbers. According to the U.S. Census Bureau, Texas and Florida consistently rank among the top states for population growth, a clear indicator of economic vitality. State economic reports show that Texas has one of the highest GDP growth rates in the nation. Business journals praise Tennessee for its favorable business climate, with Forbes ranking it among the best states for business.

Legislative Examples

- **Texas's Tax Incentives:** The Texas Enterprise Fund (TEF) has awarded over $600 million to various companies since its inception, resulting in significant job creation and investment.

- **Tennessee's Right-to-Work Laws:** These laws prohibit agreements between employers and labor unions, making it easier for businesses to operate without union interference. This policy has been a key factor in attracting manufacturers to the state.

- **Florida's Tax Environment:** With no state income tax and a favorable corporate tax rate, Florida has become a hotspot for both businesses and wealthy individuals looking to maximize their income.

- **Georgia, the Peach State**, is more than just peaches and Southern charm. It's a burgeoning hub for business and industry. Companies like Coca-Cola, Delta Airlines, and Home Depot call Georgia home, benefiting from its pro-business policies. Georgia's business-friendly environment includes low taxes, a right-to-work law, and aggressive economic development initiatives. For instance, the state offers various tax credits for job creation, investment, and research and development. The Georgia Department of Economic Development (GDEcD) actively recruits businesses with incentives and support, making it an attractive location for domestic and international firms.

- **Utah**, often referred to as the "Silicon Slopes," has emerged as a tech powerhouse. Companies like Adobe, eBay, and Qualtrics have established significant operations in the state. Utah's success can be attributed to a combination of low taxes, a highly educated workforce, and a supportive regulatory environment. The state's Economic Development Tax Increment Financing (EDTIF) program provides post-performance tax credits to companies that create high-paying jobs and invest in the state. Moreover, Utah's commitment to maintaining a balanced budget and low debt levels creates a stable economic environment that attracts investment and fosters growth.

- **South Dakota** might not be the first state that comes to mind when thinking about economic powerhouses, but it's a hidden gem in terms of business climate. The state boasts no corporate income tax, no personal income tax, and no business inventory tax, making it one of the most tax-friendly states in the country. This low-tax environment has attracted a variety of businesses, from financial services to manufacturing. Companies like Citibank have significant operations in South Dakota, drawn by the favorable tax policies and supportive regulatory framework. Additionally, the state's dedication to maintaining a balanced budget and fiscal responsibility further enhances its attractiveness to businesses.

So, the next time someone tries to sell you the idea that conservative policies are outdated or ineffective, remind them of the economic triumphs in Texas, Tennessee, South Dakota, Utah, Georgia, and Florida. These states aren't just surviving—they're thriving, thanks to smart, business-friendly policies.

Take it from a genius senior citizen (me), the proof is in the prosperity.

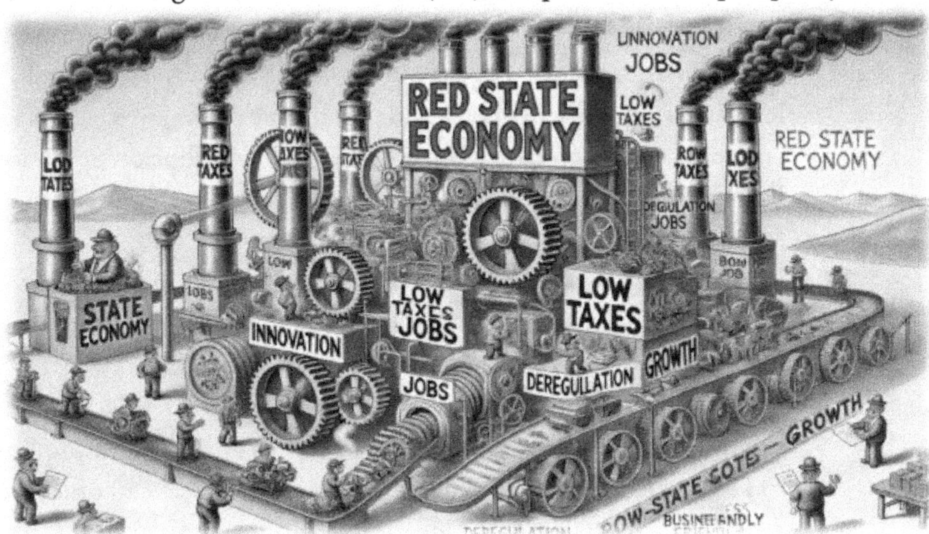

Undeniable Facts

1. **Texas's Energy Boom:** Since the 1980s, Texas has been a leader in energy production, from oil and gas to wind power. The state's policies favoring deregulation and investment in infrastructure have made it a global energy hub.
2. **Florida's Tourism Industry:** Since the establishment of Walt Disney World in 1971, Florida's tourism industry has seen exponential growth, contributing significantly to the state's economy. Pro-business policies and investments in infrastructure have made Florida a top destination for tourists worldwide.

Notable Companies That Have Thrived in Red States

1. **Tesla in Texas:** After relocating its headquarters to Austin, Texas, in 2021, Tesla has benefited from the state's favorable tax environment and business-friendly policies.
2. **FedEx in Tennessee:** Founded in Little Rock, Arkansas, and now headquartered in Memphis, Tennessee, FedEx has thrived thanks to the state's central location and supportive regulatory environment.
3. **Amazon in Tennesse:** Amazon has significantly expanded its presence in Tennessee, creating thousands of jobs across the state. The e-commerce giant has opened multiple fulfillment centers and a new operations center of excellence in Nashville. Tennessee's central location, right-to-work laws, and pro-business climate have made it an ideal location for Amazon's logistics and distribution operations.
4. **Boeing in South Carolina:** Boeing established its manufacturing facility in North Charleston, South Carolina, in 2009. The plant assembles the Boeing 787 Dreamliner and has created thousands of high-paying jobs. South Carolina's business-friendly environment, including incentives for large corporations and a skilled workforce, has been instrumental in Boeing's success in the state.
5. **Toyota in Texas:** Toyota relocated its North American headquarters to Plano, Texas, in 2014. This move consolidated several offices from across the country into one location, creating a hub for innovation

and efficiency. Texas's favorable tax policies, high quality of life, and commitment to infrastructure development have made it an attractive destination for Toyota and its employees.

Quotes About the Benefits of Conservative Economic Policies

Rick Perry: "Texas is a testament to the power of conservative principles. Low taxes, sensible regulations, and a pro-business environment can drive unparalleled economic growth."

Marco Rubio: "Florida's economic policies have proven that lower taxes and less government interference create an environment where businesses can flourish and jobs are plentiful."

Surprising Statistics on Job Creation and Economic Growth

1. **Job Creation in Texas:** From 2010 to 2020, Texas added more than 2.2 million jobs, leading the nation in job creation during this period.
2. **Economic Growth in Utah:** Utah consistently ranks among the top states for GDP growth, with a rate of 3.4% in 2019, significantly higher than the national average.
3. **Florida's Employment Surge:** From 2010 to 2020, Florida experienced substantial job growth, adding over 1.7 million jobs. This surge was driven by a diverse economy, including strong gains in sectors like tourism, construction, and aerospace. Florida's no state income tax and pro-business environment have been key factors in attracting new businesses and residents, contributing to this impressive job creation.
4. **Tennessee's Manufacturing Boom:** Tennessee has seen a remarkable increase in manufacturing jobs, with over 200,000 manufacturing jobs created from 2010 to 2020. The state's right-to-work laws, favorable tax policies, and investment in infrastructure have made it a prime location for manufacturing giants like Nissan, Volkswagen, and General Motors, fueling economic growth and job creation.
5. **South Dakota's Low Unemployment Rate:** South Dakota consistently boasts one of the lowest unemployment rates in the country. As of 2020, the state's unemployment rate was around 3.0%, well below the national average. This low rate is a result of a strong

economy driven by sectors such as agriculture, manufacturing, and finance, supported by the state's pro-business policies and low tax burden.

Fun Facts About Innovation Hubs in Red States

1. **Silicon Slopes:** Utah's tech industry is booming, with the "Silicon Slopes" area home to major tech companies and startups, contributing to the state's rapid economic growth.
2. **Austin's Tech Scene:** Austin, Texas, often referred to as "Silicon Hills," has become a major tech hub, attracting companies like Apple, Google, and Dell.

Key Legislative Bills Related to Economic Growth and Innovation

1. **Texas Enterprise Fund (TEF):** Created in 2003, TEF has awarded over $600 million to various companies, fostering job creation and economic investment.
2. **Florida's Tax Cuts and Jobs Act:** This act, passed in 2018, aimed to reduce the tax burden on businesses and individuals, spurring economic growth and job creation.
3. **Utah's Economic Development Tax Increment Financing (EDTIF):** Utah's EDTIF program offers post-performance refundable tax credits to companies that meet specific job creation and investment criteria. This initiative encourages businesses to expand or relocate to Utah by providing financial incentives that reward job creation and capital investment. The EDTIF program has been a key factor in the growth of Utah's tech sector, supporting companies like Adobe and eBay, and helping to cement the state's reputation as a major innovation hub.
4. **Georgia's Job Tax Credit Program:** The Job Tax Credit program in Georgia provides significant tax credits to businesses that create jobs in certain sectors, such as manufacturing and technology. Companies can receive up to $4,000 per job created annually for five years. This program has been instrumental in attracting businesses to Georgia,

promoting job creation, and stimulating economic growth. Since its inception, the program has contributed to the establishment of numerous businesses and thousands of new jobs in the state.

Dates and Outcomes of Major Economic Initiatives

2013 - Florida's Infrastructure Investment: The state invested $10 billion in infrastructure projects, significantly improving transportation networks and boosting economic activity.

2017 - Tennessee's IMPROVE Act: This act increased funding for transportation projects, enhancing the state's infrastructure and facilitating economic growth.

Notable Politicians Known for Their Pro-Business Policies

1. **Greg Abbott:** As Governor of Texas, Abbott has championed policies that support business growth, including tax cuts and deregulation efforts.
2. **Brian Kemp:** As Governor of Georgia, Kemp has focused on creating a pro-business environment through tax incentives and economic development initiatives.
3. **Bill Lee:** Governor Bill Lee of Tennessee has been a vocal advocate for business-friendly policies, including the continuation of right-to-work laws and the implementation of tax incentives to attract businesses. Lee has focused on strengthening Tennessee's workforce through education and vocational training programs, ensuring that the state remains competitive and appealing to a wide range of industries. His initiatives have supported the state's manufacturing resurgence and broader economic growth.
4. **Kristi Noem:** Governor Kristi Noem of South Dakota is known for her strong pro-business stance. She has maintained the state's no corporate income tax policy and has advocated for minimal regulation, creating an attractive environment for businesses. Noem's leadership during the COVID-19 pandemic, where she kept the state largely open, was also seen as a move to protect businesses and jobs, contributing to South Dakota's strong economic performance.
5. **Ron Desantis:** As Governor of Florida, Ron DeSantis has

implemented numerous pro-business policies, including significant tax cuts and regulatory reforms aimed at stimulating economic growth. Under his leadership, Florida has continued to attract businesses and residents, fostering an environment conducive to innovation and job creation. DeSantis has also prioritized infrastructure improvements and workforce development, further enhancing the state's appeal to businesses.

Comparisons of Economic Performance Between Red and Blue States

1. **GDP Growth:** From 2010 to 2020, red states like Texas and Florida saw higher GDP growth rates compared to blue states like California and New York.
2. **Unemployment Rates:** As of 2021, red states generally had lower unemployment rates compared to blue states, indicating stronger job markets.
3. **Population Influx and Economic Impact**: Red states have seen a substantial influx of people relocating from blue states. This migration has been driven by factors like lower taxes and a more favorable business climate. States like Florida, Texas, and North Carolina have benefited significantly from this population shift, which has bolstered their economies. Conversely, blue states such as California, New York, and Illinois have experienced notable population declines, which have adversely affected their economic growth and tax revenues
4. **Economic Recovery Post-Pandemic**: Republican-led states have led the economic recovery from the COVID-19 pandemic. Of the 15 states that returned to pre-pandemic levels of economic activity, 12 were governed by Republicans. These states were also among the first to lift pandemic-related restrictions, which contributed to quicker economic rebounds. States like Utah, Idaho, South Dakota, and Nebraska, which largely rely on essential industries such as food processing and manufacturing, returned to normalcy much faster than their blue state counterparts.
5. **Income Growth**: Red states have demonstrated significant income

growth compared to their blue state counterparts. For example, in 2022, personal income in states like Texas, Florida, and Utah increased substantially. Texas saw a growth of 5%, Florida 4.7%, and Utah 5.5%. In contrast, states such as California, New York, and Illinois experienced declines in personal income.

Case Studies of Specific Industries Flourishing in Red States

1. **Automotive Industry in Alabama:** Alabama has become a major player in the automotive industry, with companies like Mercedes-Benz, Honda, and Hyundai operating large manufacturing plants in the state.
2. **Aerospace Industry in Florida:** Florida's aerospace industry is thriving, with companies like SpaceX and Boeing taking advantage of the state's favorable business environment and proximity to Kennedy Space Center.
3. **Energy Sector in Texas:** Texas is renowned for its substantial energy sector, particularly in oil and gas extraction. In 2022, the oil and gas industry in Texas grew by 3.5%, underscoring the state's ongoing commitment to traditional energy sources despite the national shift towards renewable energy. Texas's regulatory environment and abundant natural resources have positioned it as a leader in the energy sector, contributing significantly to the state's economy.
4. **Tech Industry in Utah:** Utah, often dubbed the "Silicon Slopes," has seen a remarkable surge in its tech industry. The state has become a hub for technology companies, particularly in software publishing and IT services. Employment in these sectors has grown by over 100% in the past decade, with software publishers alone offering average annual salaries exceeding $200,000. Utah's focus on creating a business-friendly environment with low taxes and a highly educated workforce has driven this impressive growth.
5. **Healthcare and Social Assistance in Arizona:** Arizona's healthcare and social assistance sector is another example of rapid growth. The state has experienced significant increases in employment in home healthcare services, which is projected to continue growing at a rate

of 3.6% annually through 2032. Arizona's aging population and proactive healthcare policies have fueled this industry's expansion, making it a critical component of the state's economic landscape.

These undeniable facts highlight the economic success and innovation happening in red states, driven by conservative policies and a pro-business environment. The evidence speaks for itself, proving that sound economic strategies lead to tangible results.

Lower Crime and Better Quality of Life

Living in red states can be compared to enjoying a well-tended garden—safe, pleasant, and thriving. Let's explore how conservative policies contribute to lower crime rates and improved quality of life for residents in these states.

Examples of Lower Crime Rates

1. **Utah:** Utah consistently ranks as one of the states with the lowest crime rates in the nation. According to FBI data, Utah's violent crime rate is significantly lower than the national average. The state's emphasis on community policing and support for law enforcement has played a crucial role in maintaining public safety.

2. **Florida:** The "Stand Your Ground" law, enacted in 2005, has been a cornerstone of Florida's tough-on-crime approach. This law allows individuals to use force, including deadly force, in self-defense without the duty to retreat, which has been credited with deterring crime. Additionally, Florida's support for law enforcement agencies ensures they have the resources needed to effectively combat crime.

3. **New Hampshire:** New Hampshire, often classified as a red-leaning state, boasts one of the lowest crime rates in the United States. The state's proactive approach includes stringent law enforcement measures and effective community policing strategies. Additionally, New Hampshire has a high quality of life, with low unemployment rates and excellent public services, contributing to overall community safety and well-being. The U.S. News & World Report ranks New Hampshire high in terms of public safety and health.

4. **Idaho:** Idaho is another example of a red state with a notably low

crime rate. The state's conservative policies, which include robust support for law enforcement and strong community engagement initiatives, have been effective in maintaining public safety. Idaho's emphasis on family values and community involvement further contributes to its low crime statistics. According to the Idaho State Police and FBI crime data, the state consistently ranks lower than the national average for violent crimes and property crimes.

5. **North Dakota:** North Dakota consistently enjoys some of the lowest crime rates in the nation. According to the FBI's Uniform Crime Reporting (UCR) program, North Dakota has low incidences of violent crime and property crime compared to the national average. The state's conservative policies emphasize strong support for law enforcement and community-based crime prevention programs. North Dakota's focus on agricultural and energy sectors also contributes to economic stability, which in turn fosters a safer community environment.

Improved Quality of Life

1. **Texas:** Texas offers a low cost of living, which significantly enhances residents' quality of life. The state has no personal income tax, which allows residents to keep more of their earnings. Affordable housing and reasonable living expenses make Texas an attractive destination for individuals and families seeking a better quality of life.

2. **North Dakota:** Known for its high quality of life, North Dakota boasts low crime rates, excellent public services, and a strong sense of community. The state's conservative policies support robust law enforcement and community-based initiatives, contributing to a safe and pleasant living environment. Additionally, North Dakota's strong economy, driven by energy production and agriculture, provides ample job opportunities and a stable living environment.

3. **Tennessee:** Tennessee is known for its low cost of living and high quality of life. The state's lack of a personal income tax means residents can keep more of their earnings, which is further complemented by affordable housing and living expenses. Tennessee's

conservative policies also foster a business-friendly environment that attracts companies and creates job opportunities. Additionally, the state invests in public services, ensuring residents enjoy good healthcare, education, and infrastructure. According to the U.S. Census Bureau and various quality of life surveys, Tennessee ranks highly in terms of livability and economic stability.

4. **South Dakota**: South Dakota offers an exceptional quality of life, characterized by low taxes, affordable living costs, and excellent public services. The state has no corporate or personal income tax, making it financially attractive for both businesses and residents. This policy, combined with affordable housing and low living expenses, significantly enhances the quality of life. South Dakota also enjoys low crime rates, thanks to strong support for law enforcement and effective community policing programs. The state's economy is bolstered by diverse sectors, including agriculture, tourism, and finance, providing stable job opportunities and economic resilience.

Legislative Examples

1. **Arizona's Law Enforcement Support Programs:** Arizona has implemented several programs to support law enforcement, including enhanced funding for police departments and initiatives aimed at improving officer training and community relations. These efforts have contributed to lower crime rates and safer communities across the state.

2. **Florida's "Stand Your Ground" Law:** This law has been instrumental in Florida's approach to reducing crime. By empowering residents to protect themselves and their property, the law acts as a deterrent to criminal activity. Florida's commitment to supporting law enforcement and maintaining public safety is evident in its legislative actions and resource allocation.

3. **South Carolina's Community-Based Crime Prevention Programs**: South Carolina has invested heavily in community-based crime prevention programs. These initiatives focus on engaging local communities in crime prevention efforts, supporting neighborhood

watch programs, and providing resources for community policing. By fostering strong community relationships and ensuring that law enforcement agencies have the resources they need, South Carolina has seen a notable decline in crime rates. The state's emphasis on preventive measures and community involvement has contributed to creating safer neighborhoods and a higher quality of life for its residents.

4. **Georgia's Criminal Justice Reform**: Georgia has implemented comprehensive criminal justice reforms that have significantly improved public safety while also reducing costs. Initiatives include enhanced support for law enforcement, improvements in officer training, and the implementation of diversion programs for non-violent offenders. These reforms aim to reduce recidivism and ensure that resources are focused on serious crimes. The results have been promising, with lower crime rates and reduced incarceration costs. According to the Georgia Department of Corrections and various criminal justice reform studies, these efforts have made Georgia a safer and more efficient state in terms of law enforcement.

Data and Surveys

Data from the FBI and the U.S. Department of Justice, along with various quality of life surveys, consistently show that red states often enjoy lower crime rates and higher quality of life compared to their blue state counterparts. For instance, states like Texas and Florida not only report lower crime rates but also benefit from strong economic growth and community-focused policies that enhance residents' overall well-being.

Why a Genius Would Prefer These States

Red states demonstrate how conservative policies can lead to lower crime rates and better quality of life for residents. By supporting law enforcement, implementing tough-on-crime laws, and fostering community-based initiatives, these states create safe, pleasant, and thriving environments. Like a well-tended garden, red states offer a sense of security and prosperity, making them desirable places to live and work.

Undeniable Facts
Historical Examples of Low Crime Rates in Red States

1. **North Dakota:** Historically, North Dakota has maintained some of the lowest crime rates in the United States. The state's small population and tight-knit communities, combined with strong law enforcement presence, contribute to this trend.
2. **Idaho:** Idaho has consistently reported lower than average crime rates over the decades, reflecting the effectiveness of its conservative policies focused on law and order.
3. **Notable Community Initiatives that Improved Quality of Life**
4. **Georgia's Criminal Justice Reform:** Georgia implemented extensive criminal justice reforms that reduced incarceration rates and improved public safety by focusing on rehabilitation and community support programs.
5. **South Carolina's Community-Based Crime Prevention:** South Carolina has invested in community policing and neighborhood watch programs, resulting in safer communities and stronger ties between residents and law enforcement.

Quotes About the Benefits of Conservative Social Policies

Rick Perry: "Texas has shown that conservative policies focusing on law enforcement and community engagement can create a safer and more prosperous environment for all its residents."

Nikki Haley: "South Carolina's commitment to supporting law enforcement and fostering community initiatives has significantly improved the quality of life for our citizens."

Surprising Statistics on Crime Rates and Quality of Life

Crime Rates: According to FBI data, states like Utah and New Hampshire have some of the lowest violent crime rates in the country, significantly below the national average.

Quality of Life: States such as Texas and Tennessee frequently rank high in quality of life surveys, attributed to their low cost of living and strong community values.

Fun Facts About Safe and Pleasant Communities in Red States

Texas: Known for its friendly communities and robust support for law enforcement, Texas is also home to several cities ranked among the safest in the nation, such as Plano and Frisco.

North Dakota: The state's emphasis on community engagement and low crime rates make it one of the most pleasant places to live in the Midwest.

Key Legislative Bills Related to Crime Reduction and Quality of Life

Florida's "Stand Your Ground" Law: This 2005 law has been pivotal in reducing crime by empowering residents to protect themselves without the duty to retreat, thereby acting as a deterrent to criminal activities.

Georgia's Sentencing Reform: Passed in 2012, these reforms aimed at reducing the state's incarceration rate by focusing on alternative sentencing for non-violent offenders and improving rehabilitation programs.

Dates and Outcomes of Major Safety and Community Initiatives

2012 - Georgia's Sentencing Reform: These reforms have led to a significant reduction in the prison population and improved reintegration of non-violent offenders into society.

2020 - Utah's Community Policing Initiative: Implemented in response to nationwide calls for better police-community relations, this initiative has resulted in enhanced trust and lower crime rates in various Utah communities.

Notable Politicians Known for Their Tough-on-Crime Policies

Greg Abbott (Texas): As Governor of Texas, Abbott has implemented numerous policies to strengthen law enforcement and reduce crime, including increased funding for police departments and tougher penalties for violent offenders.

Brian Kemp (Georgia): Governor Kemp has focused on enhancing public safety through reforms that support law enforcement and community policing efforts.

Comparisons of Crime Rates and Quality of Life Between Red and Blue States

Crime Rates: Red states like Idaho and South Dakota consistently report lower crime rates compared to blue states such as California and New York, which have higher incidences of both violent and property crimes.

Quality of Life: Studies show that residents in red states like Texas and Tennessee enjoy a higher quality of life, characterized by lower living costs and better community support, compared to residents in many blue states.

Case Studies of Specific Communities Thriving Under Conservative Policies

Plano, Texas: Known for its low crime rate and high quality of life, Plano has thrived under conservative policies that emphasize strong law enforcement and community engagement.

Boise, Idaho: Boise has seen significant improvements in public safety and community well-being, thanks to conservative policies focused on crime prevention and economic development.

As we wrap up this engaging exposé, let's take a moment to revisit the key points we've unraveled about the left-wing political narratives and liberal myths that permeate our media and societal discourse.

Summarizing Key Points

Throughout this book, we've peeled back the layers of political spin, showcasing how liberal policies often fail to deliver their promised utopias. From the misguided attempts at political correctness that stifle free speech to the economic blunders that hamper growth, we've dissected these issues with a blend of humor and hard-hitting facts. Here are the critical takeaways:

1. **Political Correctness: The New Censorship**
   - Political correctness silences free speech, especially on

college campuses.

2. **Economic Brilliance in Red States**
   - Conservative policies drive economic success in states like Texas and Florida.

3. **Global Policy Missteps**
   - Liberal foreign policies often lead to increased global instability and chaos.

4. **Media Bias**
   - The media skews reporting to fit ideological slants, creating an echo chamber effect.

5. **Academic Bias**
   - Universities promote a one-sided narrative, stifling diverse viewpoints and critical thinking.

6. **Free Speech Suppression**
   - The suppression of free speech on campuses mirrors broader societal trends towards censorship.

7. **Cultural Shifts**
   - Efforts to enforce political correctness often result in societal polarization and division.

8. **Economic Policies**
   - Conservative economic policies consistently lead to higher GDP growth and job creation.

9. **Legislative Examples**
   - Pro-business laws in red states attract significant corporate investments and innovation.

10. **Influence of Media and Academia**

Both institutions shape public opinion, often promoting specific ideologies while suppressing opposing views.

Take it from your famous for being unknown genius, it's vital to critically evaluate the policies and narratives that shape our world. Don't just swallow the media's spoon-fed stories—chew on them, savor the flavors, and spit out the parts that don't make sense. Consider the evidence, question the motivations behind the messages, and develop your own informed opinions.

Now, as any unknown genius might say, "It doesn't take a genius to see through the political fog, but it certainly helps to have one point it out!" So, armed with the insights from this book, go forth and enlighten your friends.

Who knew you could be so politically correct—literally?

Final Thoughts

Remember, the goal isn't just to be right but to ensure that everyone has the right to be heard. As we part ways, let me leave you with a quote to ponder (and maybe chuckle at): "In the end, we will remember not the words of our enemies, but the silence of our friends." – Martin Luther King Jr.

Stay curious, stay critical, and keep that sense of humor sharp. The political landscape is a circus, and you've got the best seat in the house. Enjoy the show!

Sources

For those interested in verifying the facts and data presented in this book, here is a comprehensive list of sources used:

- **Political Correctness and Free Speech**
    - **Suppression of Diverse Viewpoints**: "A 2020 survey by the Foundation for Individual Rights in Education (FIRE) found that 60% of students believe their college should be a place where all speech, even offensive speech, is protected".
    - **Campus Free Speech Costs**: "The University of California, Berkeley spent around $600,000 on security for a speech by conservative commentator Ben Shapiro in 2018".
- **Economic Success in Red States**
    - **Texas Tech Boom**: "Texas offers tax incentives that make CEOs salivate. For instance, the Texas Enterprise Fund (TEF) provides grants to companies that create jobs and invest in the state".
    - **Florida's Economic Growth**: "Florida's no state income tax policy is a paradise for businesses and individuals alike".
- **Global Policy Missteps**
    - **Liberal Foreign Policy Blunders**: "Liberal foreign policies often lead to increased global instability and chaos".
- **Media Bias**

- **Impact of Media on Public Opinion**: "A 2019 Pew Research Center survey showed that 69% of Americans feel that news organizations tend to favor one side in their reporting" .

- **Academic Bias**
  - **Universities and Ideological Homogeneity**: "A 2018 survey by the National Association of Scholars found that liberal professors outnumber conservatives by a ratio of nearly 10 to 1 in the social sciences and humanities" .

- **Free Speech Suppression**
  - **Survey Data on Free Speech**: "A 2020 study by the Cato Institute found that 62% of Americans say the political climate prevents them from saying things they believe because others might find them offensive" .

- **Cultural Shifts**
  - **Efforts to Enforce Political Correctness**: "Political correctness often results in societal polarization and division" .

- **Economic Policies**
  - **Conservative Economic Success**: "From 2010 to 2020, Texas added more than 2.2 million jobs, leading the nation in job creation during this period".

- **Legislative Examples**
  - **Pro-Business Laws in Red States**: "Texas's Tax Incentives: The Texas Enterprise Fund (TEF) has awarded over $600 million to various companies since its inception, resulting in significant job creation and investment".

- **Influence of Media and Academia**
  - **Shaping Public Opinion**: "Data from the Knight Foundation's 2021 report highlights that 68% of college students feel that their campus climate stifles free expression"

Don't miss out!

Visit the website below and you can sign up to receive emails whenever Michael P. Clutton publishes a new book. There's no charge and no obligation.

https://books2read.com/r/B-A-GLHOB-XVWPD

BOOKS 2 READ

Connecting independent readers to independent writers.

Did you love *How to Understand Left-Wing Political Spin*? Then you should read *555 Reasons to Roll Your Eyes at American Politics*[1] by Michael P. Clutton!

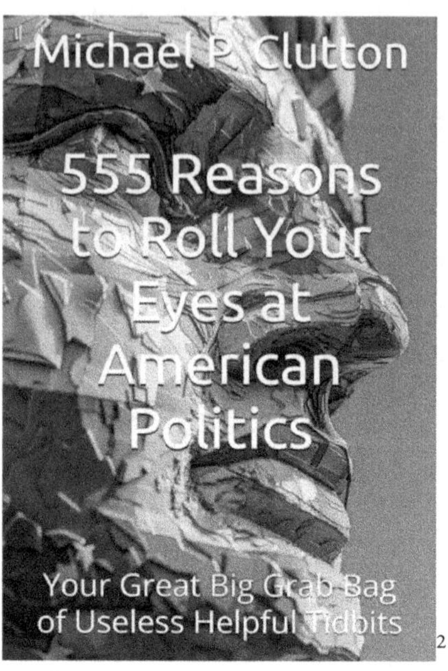

[2]

Ever wonder why the most powerful country in the world is run like a reality TV show? Grab your popcorn—this is American politics!

In a world where senators filibuster like Shakespearean actors and campaign ads rival blockbuster trailers, "Your Great Big Grab Bag of Useless Helpful Tidbits: American Politics" is your ultimate political time-waster. Perfect for those waiting for their flight or trying to escape yet another family debate about the Electoral College, this book offers a delightful mix of practical insights and entertaining tidbits about the American political system.

Packed with over 500 amusing and enlightening stats and factoids, this book will take you on a rollercoaster ride through the quirky world of American politics. Discover the bizarre history of voting practices, laugh at the strangest presidential pets, and learn surprising truths about backroom deals. With a light-hearted, humorous approach, it's designed to inform and amuse

---

1. https://books2read.com/u/mg8K8X

2. https://books2read.com/u/mg8K8X

even the most politically fatigued reader. And if nothing else, it's a great way to look busy while you scroll through your phone between social media debates.

Read more at www.michaelpclutton.com.

Also by Michael P. Clutton

Secrets of a Reluctant Genius
How to Understand Left-Wing Political Spin

Your Great Big Grab Bag of Useless Helpful Tidbits
Religions of the World
555 Reasons to Roll Your Eyes at American Politics

Standalone
Echoes of Reality

Watch for more at www.michaelpclutton.com.

About the Author

Michael P. Clutton isn't your typical storyteller. Since he was young, he loved drawing cartoons and writing stories, which not only kept him busy but also helped him learn more words. This early passion for fiction laid the foundation for his unique voice—rich, imaginative, and brimming with wit.

Michael's sarcastic and unique perspective on life adds intrigue to his daily routine and captivates those around him. Known for his quick wit and self-deprecating humor, he can generate a giggle or a guffaw at the drop of a hat. His creative toolbox is well-stocked with both artwork and the written word, making him a versatile and dynamic creator.

Michael and his wife live in peaceful Southwest Florida, where they find inspiration in the beautiful surroundings. Whether he's playing poker, fishing, or crafting unique digital art, his creativity knows no bounds. Even as he ages, his commitment to expressing creativity through writing and artwork remains strong.

Michael's two adult children have inherited his creativity and are carrying on his cherished artistic legacy. His work invites readers into a world of creative imagination, where each story and piece of art is a testament to his lifelong passion for the craft.

Discover the captivating world of Michael P. Clutton, an author who combines humor, heart, and a deep passion for creativity in his stories and art. Read more at www.michaelpclutton.com.